At Issue

| Assimilation

Other Books in the At Issue Series:

At Issue

| Assimilation

Kelly Barth, Book Editor

GREENHAVEN PRESS

A part of Gale, Cengage Learning

GALE
CENGAGE Learning™

Detroit • New York • San Francisco • New Haven, Conn • Waterville, Maine • London

Christine Nasso, *Publisher*
Elizabeth Des Chenes, *Managing Editor*

© 2010 Greenhaven Press, a part of Gale, Cengage Learning.

Gale and Greenhaven Press are registered trademarks used herein under license.

For more information, contact:
Greenhaven Press
27500 Drake Rd.
Farmington Hills, MI 48331-3535
Or you can visit our Internet site at gale.cengage.com

Articles in Greenhaven Press anthologies are often edited for length to meet page requirements. In addition, original titles of these works are changed to clearly present the main thesis and to explicitly indicate the author's opinion. Every effort is made to ensure that Greenhaven Press accurately reflects the original intent of the authors. Every effort has been made to trace the owners of copyrighted material.

Cover image © Images.com/Corbis.

LIBRARY OF CONGRESS CATALOGING-IN-PUBLICATION DATA

Assimilation / Kelly Barth, book editor.
    p. cm. -- (At issue)
    Includes bibliographical references and index.
    ISBN-13: 978-0-7377-4640-2 (hbk.)
    ISBN-13: 978-0-7377-4641-9 (pbk.)
    1. Immigrants--Cultural assimilation. 2. Assimilation (Sociology) I. Barth, Kelly.
    JV6342.A87 2009
    305.9'069120973--dc22

                             2009024280

Printed in the United States of America
1 2 3 4 5 6 7 13 12 11 10 09

Contents

Introduction

Can a person be a loyal citizen of more than one country? Is renouncing former national allegiances key to becoming an assimilated American? These questions have aroused lively debate. In one camp are those who believe holding dual citizenship prevents a person from developing patriotism and civic pride in the adopted country and from adapting to its culture. In another camp, people say dual citizenship is mostly benign and an inevitable outgrowth of an increasingly global society. They point out that until he was twenty-one years old, even President Barack Obama was a citizen of both the United States, by birth, and of Kenya, by virtue of his biological father's citizenship. Although few would question Obama's loyalty to the United States, his former Kenyan citizenship spurred renewed discussion about what makes someone wholly American.

An Exclusionary Oath?

America has always been a nation of immigrants. All but Native Americans have either descended from people who traveled here from other places or have immigrated here themselves. Over the years, however, the expectations of those who have come to call the United States home have changed. A key passage of the oath of citizenship established by Congress in 1795 required new citizens to "renounce and abjure absolutely and entirely all allegiance and fidelity to any foreign prince, potentate, state, or sovereignty of whom or which the applicant was before a subject or citizen." Though clarified somewhat over time, the oath's language still technically requires the applicant to renounce any allegiance to a foreign state.

Politicians such as President Theodore Roosevelt reinforced the exclusionary nature of this oath, demanding that immigrants speak English and adapt to the ways and beliefs of their adopted country. Rather than rebel against it, nineteenth and early twentieth century immigrants to the United States gladly abided by this interpretation of the oath. Hard-line policy was "embraced by new immigrants fleeing poverty and vicious forms of discrimination. No hyphenated Americanism, an exclusive and fierce loyalty to the new country: These were the sentiments that became dogma."[1] Though they did not renounce the customs, history, and culture of their homelands, their loyalties undeniably shifted. They found that they could retain connections to overseas relatives and settle in neighborhoods among people who shared their racial and or ethnic heritage, and yet nevertheless, claim a new identity: American.

Global Citizens

Over time, a more global attitude toward citizenship has emerged. International travel has become easier and intermarriage has become far more commonplace. Consequently, the U.S. government and immigrants themselves have moved away from this once exclusionary citizenship policy. Citizenship has come to be seen more as a right of the individual. Divided allegiances are no longer looked upon solely as obstacles to assimilation but simply as an outgrowth of modern societies. Being a citizen of two countries allows ease of travel and temporary changes in residency. It also allows immigrants to provide financial support to relatives overseas and to vote in both countries. Even though they recite the same exclusionary language in the oath, now immigrants are not officially required to renounce any previous citizenship.

This development disturbs some. America is one of few countries that permits its citizens to hold dual citizenship. Harvard University professor and immigration scholar Samuel P. Huntington believes this laxity allows immigrants to make a mockery of the oath by "falsely swearing that they are renouncing their previous allegiance, when in fact they become American citizens because they are able to maintain that previous allegiance."[2] In the past several decades, the numbers of U.S. residents holding dual citizenships has steadily increased. This signals to Huntington and other critics of U.S. immigration policy, that American citizenship has far less value than it once did. They fear this could lead to a lack of patriotism and sense of community needed to bind people together during economic crises and political strife.

Though others would concede that the attitudes of immigrants have indeed changed, they doubt that dual citizenship causes the dire consequences its critics suggest. Immigrants technically may belong in both countries, but this does not mean they feel any less invested in the health or success of either. In fact, surprisingly though many Latinos who hold dual citizenships and live near the Mexico border "celebrate their closeness to Mexico and a unique bicultural lifestyle, [they also] . . . support strong border enforcement."[3] Many people holding dual citizenship have eagerly fought for their adopted United States. Most recently, the attacks of September 11, 2001, served as a reminder to many U.S. citizens that regardless of other affiliations, they were all Americans.

Dual citizenship demands that the very word American be examined more closely. Those who would strive to keep the definition short and simple are sure to remain frustrated. Arguably, the term must encompass those whose ancestors were among the first to arrive as well as those whose lives as U.S. citizens have only just begun. It must remain elastic enough to accommodate hyphens (i.e., Cuban-Americans) and even ampersands (i.e., Korean & American). One of the greatest challenges faced by all Americans is to ensure the term "American" can stretch without breaking.

Notes

1. Nathan Glazer, "Assimilation Today," in *Reinventing the Melting Pot*, ed. Tamar Jacoby. New York: Perseus Books, 2004, p. 66.

2. Samuel P. Huntington, *Who Are We*. New York: Simon & Schuster, 2004, p. 209.

3. Gregory Rodriguez, "Mexican Americans and the Mestizo Melting Pot," in *Reinventing the Melting Pot*, ed. Tamar Jacoby. New York: Perseus Books, 2004, p. 136.

1

The United States Should Emphasize Shared Ideals

Tamar Jacoby

Professor and writer Tamar Jacoby is a member of the National Council of the Humanities. Her books include Someone Else's House: America's Unfinished Struggle for Integration *and* Reinventing the Melting Pot: The New Immigrants and What It Means to Be American.

For the United States, multiculturalism has long been an inescapable reality. However, immigrants' attitudes toward their ethnicity have changed greatly over the years. In the nineteenth and first half of the twentieth centuries, immigrants struggled to strike the delicate balance of finding their place in the culture of their adopted country while maintaining a strong sense of ethnicity. More recent arrivals have tended to identify with their racial rather than just ethnic origins, which has left them less flexibility to move out of their small groups and identify with the larger group. Sometimes this difficulty assimilating has left immigrants alienated from and even opposed to the larger culture. Though new immigrants should give up their racial and ethnic loyalties, they must adhere to some basic codes of behavior on the common ground that all Americans share. In turn, the country must acknowledge its melting pot heritage, and deemphasize the story of its white Anglo-Saxon founders.

The last forty years have brought a new kind of challenge for the traditional immigrant bargain and for American identity: multiculturalism. Welcomed by some, deplored by others, multiculturalism and the identity politics that come with it test the age-old balance from the other side, pushing seriously for the first time in our history not in the direction of conformity but for more ethnic attachment. How much difference can the American identity accommodate? Will it hold against these new pressures? Can and should it resist them? Or should it be amended, even redefined, to take account of the new emphasis we all now put on our origins? Americans have been debating these questions since the 1960s. And while this test is not yet over—these issues have hardly faded from the op-ed pages or from heated campus disputes—in the wake of 9/11 [2001], it already seems less intense, allowing us perhaps to begin to look toward a new synthesis.

There can be little question: ethnicity plays a new role in American life and will from now on. The reasons are complicated: it's not simply a new idea that took off in the 1960s and 1970s and then was spread, as some frightened observers would have it, by a few left-wing ethnic activists. Globalization, the integration of international labor markets, a more or less permanent refugee crisis, the ease of international air travel, even the maturing of the American middle class and its ever more cosmopolitan consumption habits: we live in a much smaller world than we once did and this inevitably has consequences—for American nationality and many others. Immigrants and their children now account for a full one-fifth of the U.S. population; modern communications make it much easier for them to stay in touch with their home countries. Even if ethnic studies had never been invented, many if not most of these newcomers would surely view America with a kind of "double consciousness" not unlike the one the great black man of letters, W.E.B. Du Bois, described a century ago:

"One ever feels his two-ness—an American, a Negro; two souls, two thoughts, two unreconciled strivings." Substitute "immigrant" or "Latino" or "Asian-American" for "Negro": even if multiculturalism were to disappear, few newcomers are going to outgrow this overnight, or want to, and that will inevitably mean changes for America.

Ethnicity plays a new role in American life and will from now on.

America Must Make a Place for Difference

Critics of identity politics make much of the ideological shift that fans and fuels this dual consciousness—and they aren't wrong to bemoan the excesses, intellectual and political, of the past decades. Ethnic activists with a stake in maintaining their constituencies play to exaggerated feelings of factional grievance. Misguided government policies grant benefits on the basis of race and ethnicity, spurring the establishment of permanent color-coded interest groups. Popular culture reminds people of what makes them different, not what we have in common. Corporate marketers see an easy way to score with ethnic customers, even if this means spreading stereotypes and promoting insularity. Etcetera, etcetera. Worst of all, it sometimes seems that the mainstream has lost the confidence to assert its values or to champion the American ideals that would ensure allegiance and unity. But troubling as all this is, it doesn't mean there can be no place for difference—even a somewhat more pronounced sense of difference—in American life. If history teaches anything, it's that robust ethnicity is as American as the frontier or the automobile. And today as in the past, it doesn't seem unreasonable to believe that the old American immigrant bargain will be able to contain and accommodate it.

Of course, there's difference and there's difference—some kinds more likely than others to coexist with national unity. The great-grandfather of multiculturalism, [Jewish-American philosopher] Horace Kallen himself, championed two different kinds of diversity over the course of his long career. His early writings, published in the 1920s as part of the reaction to the Americanization movement, stressed a vision of ethnicity that, he thought, neither could nor should be modified in any way as a result of contact with the American mainstream. Radically anti-assimilationist, deeply distrustful of the coercion that seemed to come with any kind of unity, this was also a vision planted firmly in racial essentialism—and it has proponents today, on both ends of the political spectrum: militant separatists *and* mainstream bigots who believe biology is destiny and cannot grasp the mystery that is *e pluribus unum* [from many, one]. Yet even Kallen eventually softened his view, never quite grasping how we as a nation might hold together, but still dropping the racialism of his early years and acknowledging the possibility that individuals can choose their identities and embrace more or less of the ethnicity they inherit.

Is Difference Ethnic or Racial?

Years later, [American sociologist] Nathan Glazer and [American ethnographer and former U.S. Senator] Daniel Patrick Moynihan made much the same point, even as they celebrated the persistence of communal difference in the 1960s and 1970s. Their classic *Beyond the Melting Pot* distinguished between two ways of embracing one's diversity: one called "ethnic," the other, more toxic in their view, "racial." (What mattered was your attitude, not your origins: both blacks and immigrants could choose either approach.) The difference was that the ethnic model allowed for choice: even if you couldn't change your color or your facial features, you could still move beyond the category you were born into—categories that, for

Glazer and Moynihan, were more about political interest than biology. What's more, unlike racial identification—which seemed already in the early 1970s to come with a heavy burden of separatism—more flexible, less demanding ethnic attachments allowed even those who felt most closely tied to the group to seize opportunities in the mainstream culture.

The perceived advantages of identity politics are not going to vanish overnight, but the only way to trump them will be to offer something better: a national identity.

Thirty years and much divisive debate later, we have new ways to talk about these different kinds of difference—and about just what makes some varieties seem more desirable than others. Nobody on either side of the discussion seems to see much problem with what is now called "symbolic ethnicity": the kind of fuzzy, feel-good diversity that surfaces generally in the third generation and feels more like a hobby than anything that could affect the outcome of one's life. Ethnic food, "roots tourism," ethnicity as folklore and nostalgia: this is what identity means now for most non-Hispanic whites, and no one thinks it threatens the nation's cohesion or identity. The harder questions have to do with the way ethnicity plays out among newer groups, and, fairly or not, this means they are posed mostly about people of color. Does this or that kind of group self-definition allow one to advance as an individual, or only as a part of a group? Does it require that one see oneself as a permanent victim? Does it lock you into a life of self-defeating anger and alienation? The social scientists' term for this is an "oppositional" identity, and no matter what your politics, it isn't hard to see how it might be harmful. Think of the black or Latino teen in an inner-city school who doesn't bother to apply himself because he thinks that's "acting white."

Can we as a nation encourage one kind of diversity and discourage the other? We won't get there through exhortation—by scolding ethnic activists or denouncing multiculturalism or trying to force-feed anyone an American identity. We've tried that kind of coercion in the past—in the early twentieth century and more recently—and it never works. On the contrary, it usually backfires, if anything increasing the alienation of the people on the receiving end. They feel singled out and put upon, and many react defensively, with the result that they ultimately feel more cut off and retreat further into their oppositional identities. The alternative is to create incentives for a more hopeful and flexible kind of ethnicity to take root. The perceived advantages of identity politics are not going to vanish overnight, but the only way to trump them will be to offer something better: a national identity that leaves room for ethnic loyalties and gives everyone, no matter what their origin, a sense that they have a stake in the larger community.

Does America Need a New Identity?

Does this mean that we as a nation need a new identity? It may. But before we take on the arduous, and possibly perilous, task of reinventing ourselves from scratch, perhaps we should look back at history and at the national identity we've inherited. The 1920s, and arguably the 1950s, gave the old bargain a bad name, but in fact it leaves lots of room for diversity, without encouraging separatism. Tested by time, tempered by previous crises, perhaps this inherited answer is still useful today. It may work just as is, or—better yet—like earlier tests, the multicultural challenge may have clarified and improved it.

What does the old identity offer someone like Eddie Liu [Asian American]? Remember, the essence, inherited from the Founding era, is a nationality that's minimal but transformative. The basic legacy—the ineluctable [inescapable] common core—is a set of ideas about how the American people should govern themselves. Like all newcomers and the native-born, Eddie must accept these basic rules of the game—the simple framework that allows us all, no matter how different, to live equitably and peaceably together. But today, as in the past, this largely political identity comes with few if any cultural corollaries. Eddie and his peers may like MTV—or they may discover [19th century American poet] Walt Whitman and fall in love with his America. Yet here, unlike, say, in France, neither kind of knowledge is required for membership: not literature, not music, not folkways, not even American food. The one cultural element that is part of the bargain is English. But even that obligation is surprisingly loose: immigrants and their children have been expected to use English in public— when they sought to participate in mainstream life—but untold millions have spoken a language other than English at home.

They or We?

If the old bargain holds, this is the line that should matter for immigrants: the line between public and private. American identity leaves ample room for all kinds of ethnicity: for communal enclaves and all that goes on there. What it does not do—or did not do in the past—was allow those divisions to play any official role in the public life of the nation as a whole. The mainstream did not traditionally formalize, sponsor or celebrate—and certainly did not pay for—ethnic attachments. The public square—whether business or government, in a mainstream school or on the job—was expected to be common ground. And when someone like Eddie ventured into the public square, he was expected to feel and act like a 100 percent American. Contemporary thinker [Director of the Center for American Common Culture at the Hudson Institute] John Fonte suggests a test for this: imagine a Korean-American schoolgirl, a child of immigrants or an immigrant herself.

When she talks about the Founders, when she recalls the Civil War, when she studies the Depression or thinks about what happened on September 11, does she think "they"—or "we"? Does she identify as an American or not? This is the transformation that the American identity requires—no more and no less than this.

The multicultural challenge has clarified but also raised questions about some of this legacy. As the identity crisis of the early twentieth century discredited the Anglo-Saxon movement and its claim that all Americans must share a common ancestry, so the ferment of the last forty years has discredited any notion that what's necessary is what social scientists call "Anglo-conformity"—identical manners. This isn't new: it's just a return to the essence of bargain. At the same time, more controversially, the multicultural era has tested the provision that the mainstream remain neutral—that it should not formalize, sponsor, celebrate or pay for ethnic divisions of any kind. Today, we do just that—in an endless variety of ways: from ethnic preferences to campus ethnic theme houses to foreign-language ballots and more. Many people oppose this, of course, and argue that we're risking dire consequences. After all, the nation is tinkering with a balance that worked, for more than two hundred years, for immigrants and the native-born. Whose interest does that serve? Does it really help newcomers to sharpen the dividing lines and emphasize what makes them different? The battle is far from over.

Our history . . . is the history of the melting pot.

Still, even those of us who deplore this reinforcing of difference and struggle against it can recognize the need felt by someone like Eddie Liu to see himself reflected in the way the nation thinks and talks about itself. What the country needs is a way to honor his dual consciousness while also strengthening his connection to America—and without compromising our commitment to a neutral public square. And here, once again, the past may have something to teach us. After all, minimal as it is, the national identity has always come with an explanatory story. As journalist and historian Michael Lind has pointed out in his important book, *The Next American Nation*, no set of abstract ideas, no matter how brilliant, can mold a nation or hold it together over the long haul. The Constitution and the Declaration of Independence alone are not what bring people to fight and die for the country. That requires a kind of attachment that is built up over a lifetime, reinforced by memories and bolstered by a rich web of shared lore: not just ideas, but beloved symbols, oft-told stories, intense common experiences and the history of how the nation's ideals worked to hold us together in the past, in crisis and in victory. What the multicultural era has reminded us is that individuals need to find a way into this history—need to see their grandfathers and grandmothers' struggles or to identify with someone who played a part something like theirs—if they are to experience that sense of "we" that is the essence of belonging. This doesn't or shouldn't necessarily mean that they can identify only with someone who looks like them. But it probably does mean that the national story has to be told somewhat differently to reflect its full complexity.

Forging an Identity as an Immigrant Country

One possibility, perhaps already taking place, would be a shift of emphasis in the national mythology to highlight the long, hard struggle that has been the forging of our national identity. This needn't mean a de-emphasis of the traditional central story, the Founding. Abraham Lincoln would remain a towering figure, the Civil War a decisive chapter. But perhaps the immigrant experience, broadly defined, should play a larger part. Not that all American history would become the history of people of color—a bitter chronicle of "us" and "them." On the contrary, it would emphasize what we all have in common: that what it means to be American is essentially to arrive as a newcomer—to start over and make a new life. From the Pilgrims to the slaves to the Ellis Island generation, this is the one experience that all Americans share: this and what follows—finding a way to fit in, or hang together, eventually by balancing your particularity against the common culture that accrued over time. Our history—indeed, some would say, the secret of our strength—is the history of the melting pot.

The new narrative would have to be written honestly. Yes, it would tell of prejudice—the hypocrisy as well as the idealism that has gone into realizing *e pluribus unum*. But it would also describe a slowly emerging tolerance and warn of excesses in both directions, including extreme forms of multiculturalism that could tear the nation apart. The cultural side of the story would be the easiest to tell: what, after all, is American popular culture if not a fossil record of the melting-pot experience—a story about hybrids and cross-pollination. Call the new narrative sensible, tempered multiculturalism: multiculturalism with a key caveat—that ultimately, although it talks about differences, it emphasizes how we coalesce as a nation. Of course, different groups of Americans, and not just ethnic groups, will want to tell it their own way, with their own highlights, and there will never be a single, "right" version. Still, in the long run, all the variants would point in the same direction: toward the shared ideals that hold us together—the ideals of tolerance, democracy and meritocracy already emphasized by our national mythology.

Is this a fundamental re-calibration of the national identity? It's a slightly different emphasis, but hardly a wholesale change. On the contrary, it could be argued, this would be a refinement of the traditional national identity: another clarification and improvement, spurred by an identity crisis, that brings out the essence of the idea. Instead of simply asserting more insistently that newcomers forget the past and drop their difference—as some alarmist opponents of multiculturalism suggest—let's tell the national story in a way that everyone can find a place in it. Assimilation happens, but ethnicity has always persisted—and if balanced against what we have in common, there's no reason it should threaten us now.

This doesn't mean that anything goes. The American identity is a big tent, but not an infinitely big tent. A young man like Eddie Liu still has to make choices—hard choices—about who he is and where his loyalties lie. He has to know that being American means something: to say that it's minimal is not the same as nonexistent. It's more than just "white-skin privilege" or a neutral framework to contain ethnic diversity. And there are limits to even the "two-way assimilation" that has made American culture the rich braid it is: American political principles—and the values that flow from them—are nonnegotiable. One can debate about whether Eddie and others like him should be allowed, as they are now, to vote in more than one country and serve in two armies—and arguably, on these points, we should insist on more complete loyalty. Still, with or without that adjustment, the traditional immigrant bargain is clear: much as we celebrate the hyphen, one side of it is more important than the other. Not only must being American come first in a foxhole; but, Eddie and his peers should also know, like it not, no matter how much they resist, in the long run, it will change them. That, history teaches, is the American way—and perhaps the meaning of being American.

2

America Must Embrace Its Melting Pot Heritage

Julia Quiroz-Martinez

Julie Quiroz-Martinez is the associate director of the Center for Third World Organizing in Oakland, California.

America has experienced many waves of anti-immigrant feeling just like the one the country experienced in the first decade of the 21st century. America has no one defined cultural heritage; all are immigrants. Legislation must be developed for immigrant issues such as state access to food stamps and welfare benefits. All Americans—those born here and new arrivals—must recommit to the idea of the country as a blend of many races and ethnicities. Citizens must not allow those from either the political right or left to lure them into opposing camps on the issue, but instead remember that we were all new immigrants to this country at one time or another in history.

For all our hard-fought alliances and hopes for unity, delving into the dynamics between immigrants and U.S.-born people of color remains a difficult and even risky proposition. These dynamics challenge us to make sense of extraordinary demographic and economic transformations, to bend our minds in new forms of analysis, and to face the delicate constructs that define our racial identity and positioning within the world.

The Color of Immigration

Prior to World War I, most immigrants to the U.S. were white and European. Many faced powerful nativist discrimination but over time joined the melting pot of American whites. Sometimes they became vociferous racists themselves in the process, like the Irish in the Chinese exclusion movement. Climbing on the racist bandwagon became a sign of Americanization—for whites.

The 1965 immigration law drastically changed the color of immigration. This law, passed on the heels of the 1964 Civil Rights Act, ended four decades of immigration quotas favoring Western Europe and significantly increased legal immigration opportunities for people from Asia and Africa. The act also placed a cap (later modified) on legal migration from the Western Hemisphere, including Latin America and the Caribbean, which increased the undocumented portion of immigration within the Americas.

Prior to World War I, most immigrants to the U.S. were white and European. Many faced powerful nativist discrimination but over time joined the melting pot of American whites.

Contemporary immigration is massive. According to the 2000 Census, there are currently 28.4 million foreign-born residents in the United States, representing 10.4 percent of the total population, mostly from Central and South America, the Caribbean, and Asia. The Census numbers also show that immigration played a major role in pushing Latinos ahead of blacks as the largest minority in the country, and in producing a remarkable new level of national origin and immigration status diversity within the black population.

These are profound demographic changes. But their political impact remains far from certain. Immigrants of color clearly have the numbers to spark a strong racial justice movement. But do we have the consciousness and strategy to seize that opportunity?

Immigrant Rights Take Off

The flow of immigrants since 1965 spurred the formation of organizations that sought to protect their rights. Focusing primarily on immigration policy, these groups led community-based campaigns to stop the Simpson-Mazzoli bill [incorporated into the Immigration Reform and Control Act] of the early '80s, and to oppose the punitive measures of the Immigration Reform and Control Act (IRCA) in 1986. With IRCA's amnesty provisions, four million undocumented immigrants living in the United States became eligible to enter the years-long process of legalizing and potentially becoming citizens. Thus began the development of an immigrant rights infrastructure heavily based in helping immigrants to become legal and, for some organizations, continuing to fight to protect and expand the rights of those who are not.

Contemporary immigration is massive.

Understandably, immigrant rights organizing has focused on those issues and institutions that make and enforce immigration law: the INS [U.S. Immigration and Naturalizaton Service, whose services were transferred into the Dept. of Homeland Security in March 2003], the border patrol, employer sanctions, immigration policy, legalization, foreign relations, and language rights. This organizing has often remained isolated from fights for racial justice. Similarly, racial justice campaigns—such as exposing and remedying discrimination in housing, employment, education, law enforcement, insurance and bank redlining, and toxic dumping—focus on the principal institutions of racism, and have seldom incorporated demands for "immigrant rights"—even when centered in immigrant communities.

"The same immigrants who didn't have papers in our communities also lived in substandard housing, were harassed by cops, and had kids in neglected schools. But we thought that fixing immigration status was someone else's job. 'That's for the lawyers on the other side of town,'" observes Juan Leyton, a Chilean immigrant and long-time organizer in Roxbury, who now runs La Vida Urbana in Boston. "Looking back at it, we failed to account for the totality of our members' experiences. They were discriminated against by racist housing policies, and were easily exploited by landlords because they didn't have papers."

Immigrant rights organizations were also trying to keep up with the explosion of amnesty applicants from the 1986 law, and received and spent resources running service programs to take advantage of the space that law created. Pancho Arguelles, an immigrant rights activist from Houston who now coordinates the National Organizers Alliance's Immigrant Community Organizers Working Group, recalls: "We took a service approach to respond to the new situation. On the one hand, we had to meet the urgent needs of our base. But in adopting this approach, we built a dependency in treating folks as clients, rather than organizing them to become active in all the issues that affected them. We missed an opportunity to link their oppression as immigrants with their oppression as racial minorities in this country."

Recent Lessons

In 1994 the dynamic tension between race and immigration played out in California. The political fight around Proposition 187 yielded important lessons in framing an immigrant rights issue in racial justice terms. Justice-minded Californians may have lost the election (Proposition 187 won by 62 percent), but their experience may help us win future fights.

The "Illegal Aliens" measure (as the official ballot summary named the initiative, which sought to deny health care, social services, and education to the undocumented) was not originally perceived in racial justice terms. With ads portraying Latinos rampaging across the U.S.-Mexico border, its proponents framed Prop. 187 as a "reasonable" remedy to curb illegal immigration from the south. The best-funded opposition to the measure, led by white liberal political consultants, tried to defend the positive role of immigrants in the economy and society.

In the early polling, no population group, not even those most likely to be negatively affected, opposed the measure. Latinos came the closest, with 48 percent opposing Prop. 187. Both Asian Americans and African Americans heavily favored the initiative. Over time, however, these numbers changed. On election day, 77 percent of Latinos voted against the measure and were joined by 53 percent of Asian Americans and African Americans. (By contrast, white voters didn't budge, with about the same proportion—63 percent—favoring [Prop.] 187 all along.)

Grassroots campaigns to galvanize voters of color were largely credited with this electoral shift. By asking "Who's Next?" on the white supremacy hit list and emphasizing that racist authorities would inevitably scapegoat all people of color, the grassroots opposition to Prop. 187 reframed an immigrant rights issue into a fight for racial justice. By showing that Prop. 187 jeopardized the rights and well-being of all people of color, regardless of immigration status, organizers were able to greatly widen opposition to the initiative.

Emerging Opportunities

Progressives in both immigrant rights and racial justice are hoping that the current movement demanding legalization for undocumented immigrants will become an important terrain for linking race and immigration. "We need to develop some very specific anti-racist goals for legalization," argues Esmeralda Simmons. Two years ago, Simmons helped engineer an important advance when the NY Black Census 2000 Coalition, led by three black non-immigrant members of Congress, announced its opposition to the use of census data by the INS to plan raids, and its support for new policies to legalize undocumented immigrants.

Without a strong racial justice analysis, legalization proponents may fall into the trap of framing new immigrants as "model minorities": hard-working, two-parent, heterosexual families who have no need for government assistance. It's the flip side of the "welfare queen" stereotype, intended to align the material interests of immigrants with existing racial ideologies. Simmons argues, "We need to raise the question, 'Who will I become when I am naturalized and how is that feeding racism?'"

Others are watching to see whether and how organized labor will bring a racial justice consciousness to its booming new immigrant organizing. "Organized labor creates a valuable space for talking about the manipulation of workers through race and legal status," asserts Katy Nuñez-Adler, the former organizing director at the Service Employees International Union (SEIU) Local 1877 in Oakland, California, who helped lead the internal push for the AFL's [American Federation of Labor's] immigration policy reversal last February [2001]. "Workers really understand how employers try to divide them. It's not difficult for people to see." Nuñez-Adler, a Jewish California native, believes labor must "take race issues on in a more direct and systematic way," and be willing to confront taboo subjects like economic competition between U.S.-born black workers and new immigrants. Nuñez-Adler also challenges racial justice organizers to recognize the opportunity that labor presents. "There are 13.5 million union members in the United States. A real emphasis on cross-racial organizing and dialogue in labor could have big reverberations for the whole social justice movement."

Welfare reauthorization, due in 2002, may also provide organizers with the opportunity for new connections between immigrant rights and racial justice. "The 1996 welfare reform law was a real wake-up call for immigrants to see that even people with a green card could be deported and lose benefits," recalls Rini Chakraborty of the California Immigrant Welfare Collaborative. "Welfare issues offer immigrants a gateway to understanding oppression that is not based on immigration status."

Chakraborty believes that welfare rights organizing on issues such as federal restoration of benefits, state access to food stamps, and language discrimination can build the link between national origin oppression and racial oppression by emphasizing that "the targets of the 1996 law were people of color. In its intent and its impact, the law was blatantly racist and anti-immigrant."

Why We Need Each Other

Obviously, the gap between immigrant rights and racial justice offers the right a huge and powerful wedge. But the mutual self-interest doesn't end there.

Without a well-developed racial justice consciousness and set of organizing strategies, immigrant rights could devolve into racist and ultimately self-defeating assimilationism. And without a strong global migration analysis, racial justice is likely to stagnate within a myopic and artificial domestic framework that neglects huge numbers of people of color.

Finally, all of us need to take a long, hard look at painful dynamics such as tension between U.S.-born and foreign-born people of African descent, racial hierarchies among Latinos, nationality distinctions among Asians, and legal immigrants' hostility toward undocumented immigrants. Unless they are connected, immigrant rights and racial justice will stumble on their own internal contradictions, shattering the heart of our movements, our families, and our selves.

3

Assimilation Brings Lower Status for Minorities

Aviva Chomsky

Aviva Chomsky is a professor and coordinator of Latin American Studies at Salem State College in Salem, Massachusetts. Her book, West Indian Workers and the United Fruit Company in Costa Rica 1870–1940, *examines the relationship between Jamaican workers and the U.S. based United Fruit Company. She co-edited* The People Behind the Coal, Identity and Struggle at the Margins of the Nation-State *and* The Cuba Reader: History, Culture, Politics.

People of color have a very different immigrant experience than their white counterparts. Historically, those who were not white Anglo-Saxons, such as Europeans, assimilated by accepting the rules and identifying with white culture. They ultimately became an indistinguishable part of that culture. On the contrary, people of color, including blacks, Asians, Hispanics and Native Americans, find that when they assimilate, they do not become a part of successful America. Assimilation itself causes these people to remain impoverished and marginalized; the cultural niche awaiting them is one of low status and inequality. Even gaining an education has broadened the gap between them and similarly educated Americans.

In 1993, [African American novelist] Toni Morrison wrote, in a special issue of *Time* magazine on immigration, that the "most enduring and efficient rite of passage into American culture" for immigrants was "negative appraisals of the native-born black population. Only when the lesson of racial estrangement is learned is assimilation complete." Blacks, she said, were permanent noncitizens. "The move into mainstream America always means buying into the notion of American blacks as the real aliens."

Italian, Polish, and Jewish immigrants may not have identified with, or been accepted into, white society when they first arrived in the United States. But they, or more often their children, assimilated by becoming "white" and experienced upward mobility as they melded into the white majority. And part of the assimilation into whiteness meant the adoption of white racial attitudes.

Black Puerto Rican author Piri Thomas described the generational gap among Italians in his Bronx neighborhood in the 1940s: the mothers and grandmothers accepted him as one of their own while the new generation attacked him as a "spic [derogatory term for a Hispanic person]." . . .

[American sociologist] James Loewen points out that just as European immigrants moved out of their inner-city enclaves and merged into white America, African Americans were being residentially segregated as the phenomenon of "sundown towns," which explicitly prohibited blacks from remaining in them after the sun set, spread across the country. Assimilation for people of European origin was accompanied by ongoing exclusion of people of color already in the United States.

People of Color Who Assimilate Join a Lower Caste

For immigrants of color, assimilation means something very different than it historically has for European immigrants. For Latin American immigrants, assimilation more often means shedding their American dream and joining the lowest rungs in a caste-like society where Native Americans and African

Americans, the most "assimilated" people of color, have been consistently kept at the bottom. When Haitian immigrants assimilate, explains one study, "they become not generic, mainstream Americans but specifically African Americans and primarily the poor African Americans most vulnerable to American racism."

As Toni Morrison suggested, racial inequality is so deeply embedded in the national culture and social fabric of the United States that assimilation has historically meant finding, learning, and accepting one's place in the racial order. If new immigrants could succeed in challenging and transforming the racial order of the United States, that would be a good thing. But the signs do not point in that direction. The current anti-immigrant sentiment reinforces racial inequality.

For immigrants of color, assimilation means something very different than it historically has for European immigrants.

The United States, as we have seen, defined itself from the first as a white, Anglo-Saxon country. Africans and Native Americans may have lived in the territories claimed by the United States, but they were not citizens. The Mexicans—primarily people of Spanish and Native American origin—who were added to the U.S. population with the 1848 conquest [Mexican-American War] were granted citizenship, of a sort—but without shaking the firmly held idea that the United States was an Anglo-Saxon country.

The new, non-Anglo-Saxon immigrants, starting with the Irish in the 1850s and growing with the southern and eastern Europeans from the 1870s on, were neither Anglo-Saxons nor people of color. Many of these new European immigrants came from nations that Anglo-Saxons considered inferior, and many of them came from peoples without states. They were oppressed minorities in the countries or empires they came from. Many came from the Ottoman Empire or the Austro-Hungarian Empire. Many were Irish, from a land controlled by England, or they were Jews from Eastern Europe. Some were southern Italians, in a country only just unified, where the South was economically dependent on the North.

Europeans Assimilated Differently

When European immigrants assimilated, they joined white society in social and cultural terms. Obviously, the color of their skin did not change—but the category of "white" expanded from its former association with Anglo-Saxons to include these newcomers. Anglo-Saxonism was fundamentally based on the domination of Africans, Native Americans, and Asians, and the institutions and ideologies of the United States reflected this reality. Southern and eastern Europeans were not originally part of this racial dynamic. Assimilating into it meant accepting it and identifying with the racial inequality it entailed—insisting, successfully, on their place among whites.

Rather than leveling the playing field, educational achievement maintains or even exacerbates inequalities.

When Asian and Latino immigrants assimilate, they also assimilate to the United States racial hierarchy, but in a different way. Very few of them can cross the line into whiteness. Instead, they assimilate by becoming people of color in a racially divided society. Assimilation, instead of bringing upward mobility, brings downward mobility. Of course there are exceptions, but overwhelmingly, the social and economic statistics have told the same dreary story for many generations: blacks, Hispanics, and Native Americans are at the bottom of the social hierarchy, even—perhaps especially—those whose ancestors have the longest presence in the country. It's not lack of assimilation that keeps them marginalized—it's assimilation itself.

The relationship between assimilation and downward mobility has been especially noted in studies of school-children. Education professor Marcelo Suárez-Orozco conducted two major studies of Latino adolescents in which he found that the most recent immigrants tended to be the students with the highest aspirations and the strongest belief in the American dream. This was because, as immigrants. they were not yet educated into the U.S. racial order. Teachers consistently reported on new immigrants' commitment to education, their work ethic, and their respect for their teachers. As they became more Americanized, they entered an oppositional inner-city teenage culture that valued money, drugs, and reckless behaviors defined as cool—the opposite of the hopeful and hard-working recent arrivals.

Education Is No Longer the Key to Success

Over time new immigrants lost their optimism. They became acculturated by becoming aware of the long-standing historical place of Latinos in U.S. society. They realized that education was not the solution they had originally believed it was. In fact, studies have shown that the higher the educational level, the greater the income disparity between whites and nonwhites in U.S. society. Rather than leveling the playing field, educational achievement maintains or even exacerbates inequalities.

Although students of color may not be aware of the statistics, their decisions seem to reflect a larger awareness that education is not an automatic ticket to the American dream. A 2000 study found graduation rates to be 76 percent for white students, 57 percent for Native Americans, 55 percent for African Americans, and 53 percent for Hispanics. The newest immigrants look a lot like the oldest "foreigners" in the United States in terms of social status. Unlike whole generations of European immigrants, no amount of assimilation will ever make them white.

Like earlier generations of immigrants, those arriving today still see learning English as crucial to survival and success. But new immigrants also become aware that learning to speak English will not resolve the problems of race. Native Americans and African Americans are native speakers of English—but this has not helped them to assimilate into a U.S. society that still in many ways defines itself as white.

Of all Latino groups in the United States, it's Puerto Ricans who are the most assimilated. All Puerto Ricans have been citizens since 1917. Puerto Ricans tend to know English, and to speak English as their primary language, at much higher rates than other Latinos. Puerto Ricans also have a huge advantage over other immigrants because their citizenship status makes them eligible for public social services and gives them the automatic right to work, rights that many immigrants from other parts of Latin America lack.

Although Mexican nationals are not automatically citizens the way Puerto Ricans are, Mexicans have the longest history in the United States of any Latino group. Mexicans residing in the territories taken by the United States in 1848 were granted citizenship, and Mexicans have been migrating into the United States for a longer time than any other group.

Immigrants of color do assimilate into U.S. society, but, in contrast to white immigrants, for people of color, assimilation means downward mobility.

Yet Mexicans and Puerto Ricans have the *highest* poverty rates of any group of Latinos in the United States. Cubans, the vast majority of whom came to the United States after 1959, Dominicans, who started coming in large numbers in the 1970s, and Central Americans, whose massive migration dates to the 1980s, all have much lower poverty rates: 24.1 percent of Mexicans and 23.7 percent of Puerto Ricans in the United States lived below the poverty line in 2003, while only 14.4 percent of Cubans did.

Resisting Assimilation Yields Success

In an interesting study of black West Indian immigrants, [researcher] Mary Waters found that "immigrants and their children do better economically by maintaining a strong ethnic identity and culture and by resisting American cultural and identity influences ... those who resist becoming American do well and those who lose their immigrant ethnic distinctiveness become downwardly mobile ... When West Indians lose their distinctiveness as immigrants or ethnics they become not just Americans, but black Americans."

The picture is clear. Immigrants of color do assimilate into U.S. society, but, in contrast to white immigrants, for people of color, assimilation means downward mobility. Assimilation means learning the racial order of the United States, and for people of color it means joining the lower ranks of that racial order. The association often made between assimilation and upward mobility is based on the experience of white immigrants. For immigrants of color, the trajectory of assimilation is a very different one.

4

The Immigration Debate Must Focus on Assimilation

Robert Samuelson

Journalist Robert Samuelson has been a contributing editor at the Washington Post *since 1977. He also writes for* Newsweek, *where his columns focus on business and economic issues.*

Hispanic immigrants are not assimilating quickly or well, but neither did many of the ethnic groups who arrived in America before them. Assimilation takes a great deal of time. Nevertheless, every ethnic group must assimilate or neither they nor the United States will succeed. Neither side of the immigration debate has the right approach to the problem. Conservatives who would exact harsh penalties on existing illegal immigrants would ultimately fail to do anything but stigmatize even those Hispanics in the country legally. The liberal approach would exacerbate the economic and social problems already caused by illegal immigration by establishing guest-worker programs. The only lasting solution will involve curbing illegal immigration while at the same time helping immigrants who are already in the country illegally to become legal and assimilated citizens.

It's all about assimilation—or it should be. One of America's glories is that it has assimilated many waves of immigrants. Outsiders have become insiders. But it hasn't been easy. Every new group has struggled: Germans, Irish, Jews and Italians. All have encountered economic hardship, prejudice and discrimination. The story of U.S. immigration is often ugly. If today's wave of immigration does not end in assimilation, it will be a failure. By this standard, I think the major contending sides in the present bitter debate are leading us astray. Their proposals, if adopted, would frustrate assimilation.

On the one hand, we have the "cop" school. It adamantly opposes amnesty and would make being here illegally a felony, as opposed to a lesser crime. It toughens a variety of penalties against illegal immigrants. Elevating the seriousness of the crime would supposedly deprive them of jobs, and then illegal immigrants would return to Mexico, El Salvador or wherever. This is a pipe dream; the numbers are simply too large.

A Crackdown on Illegal Immigrants Would Be Devastating

But it is a pipe dream that, if pursued, would inflict enormous social damage. The mere threat of a crackdown stigmatizes much of the Hispanic population—whether they're legal or illegal immigrants, or whether they've been here for generations. (In 2004 there were 40 million Hispanics, says the Pew Hispanic Center; about 55 percent were estimated to be native-born, 25 percent legal immigrants and 20 percent illegal immigrants.) People feel threatened and insulted. Who wouldn't?

On the other hand we have the "guest worker" advocates. They want 400,000 or more new foreign workers annually. This would supposedly curtail illegal immigration—people who now sneak into the country could get work permits— and also cure "shortages" of unskilled American workers. Everyone wins. Not really.

We have a conspiracy against assimilation.

For starters, the term is a misnomer. Whatever the rules, most guest workers would not leave. The pull of U.S. wages (on average, almost five times what can be earned in Mexico) is too great. Moreover, there's no general shortage of unskilled workers. In March [2006] the unemployment rate of high school dropouts 25 years and older was 7 percent; since 1996, it has been below 6 percent in only two months. By contrast, the unemployment rate of college graduates in March was 2.2 percent. Given the glut of unskilled workers relative to demand, their wages often lag inflation. From 2002 to 2004, consumer prices rose 5.5 percent. Median wages rose 4.8 percent for janitors, 4.3 percent for landscapers and not at all for waitresses.

Guest Workers Cost America Money

Advocates of guest workers don't acknowledge that poor, unskilled immigrants—whether legal or illegal—create huge social costs. Every year the Census Bureau issues a report on "Income, Poverty, and Health Insurance Coverage in the United States." Here's what the 2004 report shows:

- Since 1990 the number of Hispanics with incomes below the government's poverty line has risen 52 percent; that's almost all (92 percent) of the increase in poor people.

- Among children, disparities are greater. Over the same period, Hispanic children in poverty are up 43 percent; meanwhile, the numbers of black and non-Hispanic white children in poverty declined 16.9 percent and 18.5 percent, respectively.

- Hispanics account for most (61 percent) of the increase of Americans without health insurance since 1990. The overall increase was 11.1 million; Hispanics, 6.7 million.

By most studies, poor immigrants pay less in taxes than they use in government services. As these social costs have risen, so has the backlash. Already, there's a coalition of Mayors and County Executives for Immigration Reform. It includes 63 cities, counties and towns, headed by Republicans and Democrats, ranging from Cook County, Illinois (population: 5.3 million) to Gilliam County, Oregon (population: 1,817). Coalition members want the federal government to reimburse their extra costs.

We have a conspiracy against assimilation. One side would offend and ostracize much of the Hispanic community. The other would encourage mounting social and economic costs. Either way we get a more polarized society.

On immigration, I am an optimist. We are basically a decent, open and tolerant nation. Americans respect hard work and achievement. That's why assimilation has ultimately triumphed. But I am not a foolish optimist. Assimilation requires time and the right conditions. It cannot succeed if we constantly flood the country with new, poor immigrants or embark on a vendetta against those already here.

I have argued that our policies should recognize these realities. Curb illegal immigration with true border barriers. Provide legal status (call it amnesty or whatever)—first work permits, then citizenship—for most illegal immigrants already here. Remove the job lure by imposing harsh fines against employers who hire *new* illegal immigrants. Reject big guest-worker programs.

It's sometimes said that today's Hispanics will resemble yesterday's Italians. Although they won't advance as rapidly as some other groups of more skilled immigrants, they'll still move into the mainstream. Many have—and will. But the overall analogy is a stretch, according to a recent study, "Italians Then, Mexicans Now," by sociologist Joel Perlmann of Bard College. Since 1970 wages of Mexican immigrants compared with those of native whites have declined. By contrast, wages of Italians and Poles who arrived early in the last century rose over time. For the children of immigrants, gaps are also wide. Second-generation Italians and Poles typically earned 90 percent or more compared to native whites. For second-generation Mexican Americans, the similar figure is 75 percent.

One big difference between then and now: Immigration slowly halted during and after World War I. The Italians and Poles came mainly between 1890 and 1915. Older immigrants didn't always have to compete with newcomers who beat down their wages. There was time for outsiders and insiders to adapt to each other. We should heed history's lesson.

5

A Rational Immigration Policy Is Needed to Achieve Assimilation

Paul M. Weyrich

Paul M. Weyrich is chairman and CEO of the Free Congress Foundation.

Americans have steered away from encouraging immigrants to assimilate because they instead have been told to recognize and celebrate diversity. This has hurt immigrants because it forces them into an isolated and secluded part of society. Americans' lack of patriotism has aided in the move away from assimilation, and the belief is that once American pride is restored, then immigrant assimilation will be possible and become a more pressing issue.

When my father came from Germany as a 19-year-old, the very first thing he did was to enroll in a class taught at a local public school to learn English.

My aunt told me that he became proficient in English in only six weeks. He wanted to be an American, and to do so, he had to learn the language. Of course, he retained his German heritage. However, assimilation was important to him, as it was to most immigrants.

For years America has drifted away from assimilation, which has become an unspeakable word among the cultural elite. Instead, we are told that we must recognize and celebrate the diversity of various groups without demanding any compromise from them.

This has hurt immigrants more than anyone else because many have become isolated in cultural ghettos without a proper command of English, the American political and legal systems or American history and culture.

That said, it also has fractured American society.

Decrease in Immigration Rally Attendance

For the past several years pro-illegal immigration groups have rallied at the beginning of May to demand citizenship opportunities for the estimated 12 million illegal immigrants in the United States and an end to raids on and deportations of these immigrants. This year was no different.

There were protests in California, Michigan, Florida, Texas, Illinois, and other places. One slight change, however, was the attendance: This year the protests were markedly smaller than before.

In 2006, the first year these immigration rallies were held, the attendance was around 1 million people. This year crowds were down to between 300 and 500 per rally.

Many activists were quoted as saying that the drop in attendance was due to fear of government reprisal and deportation among the illegal immigrants themselves. This is highly implausible. Since 2006 the federal government has made little progress in enforcing our borders and deporting illegal immigrants.

Political Views on Immigration and Assimilation

What worries me is that all three of the remaining presidential candidates, Sens. John S. McCain III, R-Ariz., Barack H. Obama, D-Ill., and Hillary Rodham Clinton, D-N.Y., support a general amnesty for illegal immigrants. And this amnesty is without any prior successful closure of the U.S.-Mexican border that would halt further waves of immigrants.

McCain pays lip-service to border security and assimilation on his campaign web site. He states, "A secure border will contribute to addressing our immigration problem most effectively if we also recognize the importance of a flexible labor market to keep employers in business and our economy on top, and recognize the importance of assimilation of our immigrant population, which includes learning English, American history and civics, and respecting the values of a democratic society."

Obama's Web site is similar, listing border security as his main priority, followed by "bring[ing] people out of the shadows" to become citizens. Clinton uses much more flowery language but essentially posits the same message.

It should be noted that illegal immigrants do not live in the shadows. They attend American schools, use our hospital emergency rooms as though they were a general practitioner's office and work in specific businesses.

What we need to do is return the debate to the topic of assimilation, of learning to speak English, of the value of becoming a citizen, and of pride in a country that provides immigrants from around the world with more opportunities for success than any other country on earth.

If the federal government wanted to enforce our current immigration laws, which are sufficient to solve the problem, it could. But there is no willpower to do so.

Return to Assimilation by Restoring National Pride

I suspect that the reason for the drop in attendance at the rallies is not a new burst of patriotism for America among prior attendees but because the issue is not as pressing.

What we need to do is return the debate to the topic of assimilation, of learning to speak English, of the value of becoming a citizen, and of pride in a country that provides immigrants from around the world with more opportunities for success than any other country on earth.

The latter will be the most difficult. Immigrants need to assimilate to American culture but if we are to demand that they do we must first restore a proper sense of patriotism among American citizens.

How can we demand that foreigners respect our country when our own elites so vehemently criticize and disdain everything connected to American history, culture, ideals, governance, and traditions?

A return to assimilation and a coherent culture will not begin until we put our own house in order. We cannot expect others to respect us when many Americans themselves are ashamed of their country.

6

The Melting Pot Requires Diverse Communities

Christian Science Monitor

The Christian Science Monitor *is a daily newspaper dedicated to providing international coverage of political and cultural issues using its own reporters located around the world.*

Despite all the political lauding of America's unique cultural mix, the response on the ground appears quite different. The more diverse a neighborhood, a recent study pointed out, the more frightened, distrustful and ethnically isolated its inhabitants. The study also revealed that this does not have to remain the case. As Americans learn to focus less on physical differences that can create division among people, they can become more open to the richness other ethnicities have to offer. Government at the local, state, and federal levels could learn from the ways the military and some evangelical mega-churches have brought people of vastly different backgrounds together around a common purpose.

A Supreme Court ruling Thursday [June 28, 2007] dealt a blow to schools that pick students by race to create diverse classrooms. But it didn't preclude less-racial means to achieve diversity. And it raises an old question: Is diversity good for America?

In theory, America's racial and ethnic mix can inspire idealism, based on the hope of a grand melting pot. In practice, however, it can cause many people who actually live with neighbors, students, or workers of different ethnicity or race to withdraw and retreat into their shells, producing what's called a "turtle effect."

That's the conclusion of a major new survey by an eminent scholar.

"Diversity, at least in the short run, seems to bring out the turtle in all of us," says Robert Putnam, a well-known political scientist at Harvard University and author of a massive five-year study on the effects of immigration and diversity on the United States.

Drawing on interviews with 30,000 Americans, Dr. Putnam finds that the greater the diversity in an area, the less trust neighbors have—even for those like themselves—and the more isolated they become.

That lack of trust, the study reports, shows up in a variety of ways. These residents are less likely to register to vote. They do less volunteering, give less to charity, have fewer close friends, and are less happy. They also spend more time watching television.

Finding a "shared identity that transcends differences" is a continuing effort.

The Challenges of a Diverse America Can Be Met

Yet don't be misled by the apparent challenge. Even though having different people around can be "genuinely unsettling" in the short term, Putnam is an optimist in the long run. He offers reassurance that diversity will give the US a vibrant future. He insists that it is wrong to assume that whatever tension might exist between ethnic or racial groups is a fact of life. Diversity is a challenge, not a threat.

"Over time, especially with some thought and care, we can get used to diversity," Putnam writes in *Scandinavian Political Studies*. "That's what the country has done in the past, and that's what the country is going through now."

His message of hope comes at an opportune time. As Congress wrestles with immigration, Putnam asks: How do we learn to live together to strengthen communities?

For starters, he would expand English-language training and build more community centers, playgrounds, and places to gather that can create opportunities for inclusiveness. Assimilation comes from sharing experiences, popular culture, and education. He points to the US Army and some evangelical megachurches as examples of institutions that open their doors to a variety of people and integrate them around common interests.

Ethnic and racial diversity is both inevitable and an asset. It spurs economic growth, brings new cultural influences, and increases creativity. Finding a "shared identity that transcends differences" is a continuing effort. Instead of becoming a nation of turtles, Americans will benefit by expanding their collective sense of "we" and "us."

Courts will always ask if diversity is a "compelling state interest" to justify the extent of the means to achieve it. In this latest [Supreme Court] case . . . the high court found the ends didn't justify the means.

More broadly, the more Americans define themselves above superficial physical features, the easier it will be to go beyond old debates about race and ethnicity.

7

Government Programs Keep Immigrants from Assimilating

Stanley Renshon

Stanley Renshon is a political psychologist who is coordinator of the Interdisciplinary Program in the Psychology of Social and Political Behavior at the City University of New York (CUNY) Graduate Center. His books include Political Psychology: Cultural and Cross-cultural Foundations, One America?, Political Leadership, National Identity, and the Dilemmas of Diversity, *and* America's Second Civil War: Political Leadership in a Divided Society.

Research shows that learning English is key to identifying oneself as an American. Immigrants who have strong English language skills consistently identify themselves as American or use a hyphenated identity, while those who do not learn English, identify more strongly with their country of origin. The federal government has encouraged new immigrants' reluctance to give up their strong group identity and become fully American by creating and funding business and educational programs that reward them for remaining connected to their former countries and cultures.

The abilities to speak, read, and write English are tools for successful integration into American society. Yet functional English fluency has become part of the "contested discourse" of immigration. It would seem commonsensical to view English language skills as an important tool—not only for the economic advancement of immigrants (not to mention natives) but also to help integrate immigrants into American society. Moreover, given the great weight given to "the American Creed"—a belief in and support of democracy and representative government—as well as the ability to take part in it, it would be hard to argue against the need for immigrants to learn as much English as they can, and as quickly as possible. But that is not necessarily the case.

Learning English is actually controversial. The Bilingual Education Act of 1967–68 developed by Texas senator Ralph Yarborough was specifically designed to increase English facility. It was not proposed or understood as an original-language maintenance measure, nor was its purpose to create or maintain language islands, or to create non-English dominant bilinguals. Today that specific attempt to respond to Mexican American children who are educationally at risk has spawned a vast, invested bureaucracy supported by teachers' unions and by immigration advocacy groups like MALDEF [Mexican American Defense and Education Fund] and their political allies.

Learning English is actually controversial.

Some of the same players strenuously objected when, as part of the first large general amnesty for illegal aliens, the Immigration and Reform Control Act of 1986 (IRCA), the bill's sponsors tried to include English language and civics instruction for those who wanted to become legalized. A key sponsor of this legislation, Representative Jim Wright (D-Tex.), proposed a two-year waiting period before legalization, during which candidates could work but also learn English and civics. Wright specifically eschewed the idea of a melting pot in which every different group would become mixed together in one undifferentiated whole. Rather, he wanted to give immigrants an opportunity to fit into American society in their own way. That argument won support from both liberals and conservatives and helped to break the legislative impasse that had stalled the bill. It passed Congress and was signed into law by President Ronald Reagan on November 6, 1986.

Immigration Reform Was Ultimately Watered Down

No sooner had the bill been signed than the agreements that had allowed it unraveled. Contentious debates broke out over the exact meaning of "civic instruction" for immigrants. The nature of the proposed education program and test sparked heated controversy. All questions concerning these understandings had been left to the Immigration and Naturalization Service. Money allocated for civic and language education was in turn made available to various governmental (schools, state offices) and nongovernmental (labor, religious, ethnic, and legal) organizations. Each hired its own teachers, who in turn initially determined the conditions for "satisfactory" progress and completion. Standards differed, to put it mildly.

After much debate, the content of the program was turned over to ethnic and immigrant advocacy groups. Attendance, not demonstrated competence, warranted a certificate of satisfactory completion. What had started out as a minimum of 60 hours for completion of a proposed 100-hour program floundered—critics complained that such requirements were "excessive" and "burdensome." Immigration and Naturalization Service officials finally settled on 40 course hours of a 60-hour program. The full course of instruction had been reduced by 40 percent, and the amount of time necessary to attend in order to "pass" was reduced a further 20 percent. . . .

William Kymlicka, an advocate of a "multicultural nationalism" that features specific group rights for cultural minorities, notes that "the commitment to ensure a common language has been a consistent feature of the history of [American] immigration policy." Yet he views that commitment as an insistence on "Anglo-conformity," a demand he believes should be resisted in the name of encouraging group cultural rights. Nor is he alone.

Peter Spiro, a [Temple University] law school professor, writes that "the requirement that naturalization applicants demonstrate English-language literacy presents for many the most formidable obstacle to the acquisition of citizenship." He would like to lessen the requirement and really sees no need for it. How much of a barrier is it? Even though his own figures make this unclear, Spiro claims that "naturalization law is a real instrument of exclusion and subordination." But not much analytical traction is gained by using the term "subordination," which implies domination and illegal discrimination. If that were truly the case, the United States would have to adopt an open, unrestricted admissions immigration policy.

Speak English and you are likely to self-identify as an American; identify as an American, and you will most likely be speaking English.

Speaking English Makes People American

Just how important is English-language mastery to becoming an American? More than 36,000 students were interviewed in 1980 and again in 1982 to find out whether ethnic identifications persisted, and if so why. The findings are quite clear, "Persons for whom Spanish was an important communication tool almost never (1.1%) switched [away from an ethnic identification], while English-speaking monolinguals switched to a non-Hispanic Identity at a high rate (57%)."

The same set of findings was repeated with a large survey of immigrants conducted in 1992. This survey found that among second-generation youth, those who spoke English very well were much more likely to choose a strictly American or hyphenated American identity. Those who used a language other than English with their parents or their friends were much more likely not to choose a strictly American or hyphenated American identity.

In his major survey of adolescents, [University of California sociology professor Rubén G.] Rumbaut found that "respondents who prefer English and who speak only English with their close friends are significantly more likely to identify as American, and less likely to be defined by national origin. Conversely, youths who do not prefer English and who report greater fluency in their parents' native languages are most apt to identify by national origins."

That relationship was confirmed by the Pew Hispanic study ["National Survey of Latinos"]. . . . They note that while time in the United States is associated with more of a likelihood to identify as an American, "it is only among Latinos whose families have been in the United States for multiple generations and among those who say that English is their primary language that a majority of respondents select the term 'American' as their primary identification." In other words, speak English and you are likely to self-identify as an American; identify as an American, and you will most likely be speaking English.

Hyphenated Ethnicities Add Complication

Hyphenation has a long history in the United States. It is a paradox of American ethnic identities that this country often provides more expansive identities than those with which immigrants arrived. The prototypical case is the Southern Italian worker who may have had little attachment to Italy—yet who developed that consciousness after arriving. Less remarked upon is that the same was true, to some extent, of groups like Norwegians and Swedes.

One contemporary example of this phenomenon is the designation of Latino/Latina to cover anyone who speaks Spanish, regardless of the country and culture from which they arrived. [Princeton University sociologist Douglas S.] Massey has argued, "There is no Hispanic population in the sense that there is a black population. Hispanics share no common historical memory and do not comprise a single, coherent community. Saying that someone is Hispanic or Latino reveals little or nothing about likely attitudes, behaviors, beliefs, race, religion, class or legal situation in the United States." . . .

[For example, consider] the voices from President [Bill] Clinton's One America forums. . . . Here is the voice of another immigrant, Anna Arroyo. She recalled her experience as a Puerto Rican in a college course on Latin America, indicating that her classmates thought that because of her origin she should be able to speak authoritatively on all Latin cultures. However, she said, "What people don't understand is that I'm not Peruvian; I'm not Mexican. I don't understand their culture. I'm Puerto Rican and all I know is Puerto Rico."

It is one thing for government to declare that ethnicity is acceptable and another to signal that it is preferable.

Governments Promote Group Ethnic Identity

Group attachments have always been a vehicle for socioeconomic and political advancement. City Hall facilitated the upward mobility by the Irish in Boston. Koreans and others depend on their fellow group members for employment and advancement. Group solidarity among new immigrants is as American as individualism.

Why should this be a concern now? The answer lies in the different nature of American society then and now—and in the changed role of government and policy with regard to ethnicity and identification.

Researchers generally agree that ethnic labeling by government increases the tendency of individuals so categorized to so identify. One obvious reason for this is that government commands power and prestige. If it is the government's official policy that you should consider yourself a particular kind of ethnic, then the government is sending a clear message that you should.

Immigrants can be excused if they are confused by a mixed message from the U.S. government. First, they are asked to take an oath of allegiance requiring them to renounce their former national allegiance. At the same time, they are asked to maintain their identity to their "home" country. Immigrants may well come to consider that in following the government's message to retain their group identity they are assimilating into American culture.

It is one thing for government to declare that ethnicity is acceptable and another to signal that it is preferable. American government at all levels, and many major private institutions in business and education, do more than facilitate pan-ethnic identifications—they encourage it. Many federal, state, local government, business, and education programs distribute resources on a preferential basis of ethnic and racial classifications. These include contracts, jobs, admissions to many public and private institutions, and stipends and fellowships. They thus reward individuals who make claims on the basis of group identity.

Ethnicities Are No Longer Transitional

Yet it is not only the extensiveness of preferences that makes this issue different today than in the past. Now, group identifications are no longer viewed as transitional. Let us consider the Irish and other European (Eastern and Western) ethnic groups. Yes, throughout their histories in the United States, individual members of these groups have banded together for comfort, information, and mobility. Yet as members of these groups began to branch out socially, economically, and interpersonally, through such mechanisms as cross-ethnic friendships and intermarriage, the old ties became more symbolic than practical. Today, European ethnics are more American than otherwise.

There are many reasons to question whether today's immigrants will see the uses of group membership as a transition to a more clearly identified American identity. It is basic human psychology to prefer not to give up positions that confer an advantage. The incentive structures built into ethnic identifications are powerful, and they are maintained by numerous influential and prestigious American institutions. Moreover, no reasonable timetable has ever been given for ending them voluntarily. The answer to such questions is always: Not yet—or only when discrimination has been wiped out.

There is one further difference between then and now: the fact that the integration of ethnic groups in the United States is no longer solely a matter of domestic national policy or politics. The integration of immigrants today takes place in a context in which allegiances to extranational organizations, institutions, and other countries represent an unprecedented mix of additional and potentially dangerous complications.

8

Dual Citizenship Erodes Patriotism

Bruce Fein

Bruce Fein is a constitutional lawyer and chairman of the American Freedom Agenda, an organization of conservatives committed to helping the Republican Party return to its ideological roots, including encouraging small government.

Dual citizenship causes breaches of allegiance for those who hold them. If people vote or hold office in or show significant patriotic ties to another country, they should relinquish their U.S. citizenship. Without undivided loyalty to this country, people will not embrace and serve it with the fervor and patriotism required of a citizen. When individuals are not devoted solely to the ideals of this country, they become indifferent to the culture and societal fabric of America.

The United States should end its folly of tolerating dual citizenship for persons who vote, serve in office, or otherwise demonstrate allegiance to a foreign government.

As the New Testament sermonizes, "No man can serve two masters: for either he will hate the one and love the other; or else he will hold to one, and despise the other." The United States Constitution thus prohibits any federal officeholder, without the consent of Congress, from accepting "any present, emolument [compensation], office, or title of any kind whatever, from any king, prince, or foreign state."

Most would be stunned to learn, however, that under U.S. law (8 U.S. Code, section 1481), a person may retain citizenship despite enrolling in the armed forces of a foreign nation at war with the United States, serving as president of a foreign state, or even committing treason. Raffi Hovannisian on becoming Armenia's foreign minister, declared, "I certainly do not renounce my American citizenship." Muhamed Sacirbey, foreign minister of Bosnia in 1995-1996, did not lose his U.S. citizenship. The chief of the Estonian army from 1991–1995, Aleksander Einseln, likewise enjoyed dual citizenship. As [professor and author] Thomas M. Franck has chronicled, several Americans have represented their other country of citizenship as ambassadors to the United Nations.

Last month [April 2005], the Mexican Chamber of Deputies passed legislation endowing 10 million Mexican and Mexican-Americans with the opportunity to cast absentee ballots from the United States in the 2006 Mexican presidential elections. The Central Mexican state of Zacatecas embraces Mexican migrants as candidates for electoral office. Andres Bermudez, a wealthy California grower christened the "Tomato King," captured a mayoralty. Two other immigrants garnered seats in the state legislature. Mexican candidates routinely motorcade in the U.S. seeking political support from Mexican-Americans.

Most would be stunned to learn ... that under U.S. law ... a person may retain citizenship despite enrolling in the armed forces of a foreign nation at war with the United States.

The magnitude of the dual citizenship-divided loyalty problem is elusive. Approximately 60 countries permit expatriates or migrants to vote via absentee ballots, including Venezuela, Columbia, Brazil and Honduras. The number permitting dual citizenship has been variously estimated at from 37 to 89. The U.S. government neither records nor estimates the number of its dual citizens. But baseline figures and trends are troublesome. The foreign-born population in the United States probably approaches 30 million to 35 million, or approximately 10 percent. That percentage is climbing because of disproportionate youth and high fertility.

And immigrants to the United States characteristically arrive from nations that accept dual citizenship. In sum, the problem of split allegiances cannot be swept under the rug as an inconsequential crumb.

Dual allegiances . . . fuel a yawning indifference to American customs and civic spirit indispensable to national vitality.

Patriotism is the alpha and omega of national strength, even if occasionally misappropriated as the last refuge of a scoundrel. Undivided devotion to the United States and embrace of its hallowed ideals and heroes are what make the nation flourish. Single citizenship finds expression in eagerness to enlist in the armed forces or to support its soldiers; to participate in the nation's political affairs; to join voluntary private organizations, like the Rotary Club, the League of Women Voters or the PTA; to cooperate with law enforcement; to make donations to domestic charities; and, to promote America's signature culture by living and breathing social equality, nondiscrimination, individual rights, the rule of law and freedom of speech.

Dual citizens who demonstrate political attachments to a foreign government, in contrast, will be less resolute in celebrating and advancing the interests of the United States. They will be less inclined to sacrifice to make the nation like a sparkling "city that is set on an hill," [paraphrased from President Ronald Reagan's "The Shining City Upon a Hill" speech] in the manner that Augustus Caesar "found Rome a city of bricks and left it a city of marble." Furthermore, if dual citizenship is indulged with official nonchalance, the lofty ideals associated with American citizenship will be dimmed.

Accordingly, Americans who vote in a foreign election, occupy any office in a foreign state, enlist in a foreign army, attempt to overthrow the U.S. government, or otherwise affirm allegiance to a foreign nation should forfeit their citizenship. Accomplishing that is clouded by the United States Supreme Court decision in *Afroyim v. Rusk* (1967). There, a narrow 5–4 majority held unconstitutional a statute that made voting in a political election in a foreign state a justification for revoking citizenship acquired by naturalization.

Writing for the court, Justice Hugo Black broadly sermonized that the 14th Amendment permits loss of citizenship only by voluntary relinquishment. Obeying that edict, current federal law makes a specific intent to relinquish United States nationality the touchstone for its loss.

Congress should either propose a constitutional amendment to overcome *Afroyim*; or, enact legislation that deletes the specific intent requirement in the expectation that the high court will reconsider the precedent. Dual allegiances do not imminently threaten the fabric of the United States. But they fuel a yawning indifference to American customs and civic spirit indispensable to national vitality.

9

Dual Citizenship Negates the Meaning of National Identity

Peter Spiro

Peter Spiro is a professor of international law at Temple University. His work focuses on the constitutional aspects of U.S. foreign relations and immigration and nationality law.

In the past, immigrants swore allegiance to their adopted country, officially subordinating ties to their birth country. However, with mixed marriages on the rise, the numbers of people with dual, even multiple, citizenships have increased as well. Also, people no longer rank their allegiance to one country higher than another. Though this trend might trouble some who fear that immigrants do not feel the same sense of unity and patriotism their immigrant parents and grandparents felt about the United States, such changes are inevitable in a global environment. In fact, being a citizen of a country may become more like having membership to one club among many rather than a heartfelt devotion to one homeland.

The growing incidence of plural citizenship does more than evidence the decline of citizenship, it also contributes to that decline and the decoupling of citizenship status from actual parameters of community. First, there is the "second choice" problem. In a world that demanded singular citizenship, individuals could be assumed to opt for a particular citizenship because it was their first choice. On average, that choice would reflect a balance of the sentimental ties and material benefits of one citizenship relative to another. These factors would often point in the same direction and reflect an actual priority of community membership. Thus, the naturalization decision would reflect a reprioritization of identity; the acquisition of American citizenship—accompanied by the loss of original citizenship—would (again, on average) reflect a change in the order of community ties. The old ties would not necessarily have been abandoned (in the American tradition, of course, they more often were not), but naturalization would evidence their subordination to the new affiliation. The phenomenon worked in reverse, as well. An American resettling abroad who naturalized in his new country of residence could not retain his U.S. citizenship. The naturalization would likely reflect the primacy of community ties to the other country and the subordination of ties to the United States. The result was a community in which citizenship status defined a core, because it coincided with the group for whom American identity was the first choice among national identities.

Gaining Plural Citizenship Is Easy

This construct is destroyed by the acceptance of plural citizenship, for there is no longer any implicit ranking in the citizenship choice. One can acquire citizenship in states to which one has a subordinate or even nominal ties without sacrificing one's primary attachment. This means that some citizens will sustain a substantial tie to another polity [government] in terms of their identity and commitments. That possibility may not be identity-dilutive [identity reducing], at least to the extent that identity and commitment are not zero-sum quantities. One can still be meaningfully attached to the American community at the same time that one holds more significant attachments to other nations. But plural citizenship also facilitates the citizenship of convenience. There are certain advantages to maintaining or acquiring citizenship, at the same time that obligations specific to citizenship have been reduced to virtually nothing. It is a world in which one can collect citizenships at very little cost and without any meaningful attachment to those states in which citizenship is maintained. In the near-parody version, citizenship is held for the purpose of securing access to faster passport inspection lines at airports and other ports of entry. In a world of second-, third-, even fourth-choice citizenships, the lesser ones may reflect no actual community ties.

In a world that demanded singular citizenship, individuals could be assumed to opt for a particular citizenship because it was their first choice.

Lines of Identification Blur

With the United States playing global polestar [center of attraction], the second-choice phenomenon will be more prevalent than elsewhere. As an immigrant-receiving country, there is greater probability that U.S. citizenship will either be subordinated to original citizenship . . . or acquired for the convenience and security it affords residents. One fascinating study of an extended Dominican family in New York City by sociologists Greta Gilbertson and Audrey Singer, for example, found several naturalizing as a predicate not to assimilation but to departure and return to their homeland; with American citizenship in hand, they could live in the Dominican Republic without any risk of getting cut off from relatives and better medical care in the United States. The American end of multiple citizenship facilitates transnationality, with the passport as a sort of global free pass rather than a signifier of allegiance to the American nation. And to the extent that attributes of American-ness, political and cultural, have insinuated the globe—"everyone is an American"—it will lose its distinctiveness as an identity, in which case another citizenship will particularistically define the person. To the extent that plural citizenship is normalized, America may become a community of second choicers, with a corresponding loss of filial intensity.

To the extent that plural citizenship is normalized, America may become a community of second choicers, with a corresponding loss of filial intensity.

Plural citizenship also becomes the accelerant that fuels the community-diminishing effects of birth citizenship and naturalization rules. The strong norm of singular nationality limited the extent to which other membership criteria could undermine community definition. The rule of jus soli [right of the territory] may well have extended citizenship at birth to some individuals who would not thereafter actually assimilate into the community; relaxed naturalization requirements (up until the early twentieth century, involving little more than a period of five years' residence) may have afforded citizenship to some who remained in insulated immigrant communities or who returned thereafter permanently to their homelands. But the birth citizen who ended up living her life in another national community would have forfeited her U.S. citizenship as a result of active membership in that other polity. The immigrant whose primary commitments were to his homeland would have been unlikely to exploit otherwise relaxed naturalization requirements if terminating the homeland tie remained a precondition; those who returned to their homelands lost their naturalized U.S. citizenship under the expatriation law. In short, to the extent that other citizenship rules allowed a blurring of community boundaries or a dilution of identity, the rules against dual citizenship reimposed definition and maintained intensity. Take those rules away, and the imprecision of these other conditions is fully actualized. There is no policing the happenstance birth citizen or the diasporan [people settled far from their ancestral homeland], both of whose affective and other attachments may lie elsewhere.

The notion of imprecision points to plural citizenship's assault on citizenship as a primary locus of identity. If one paints the question as one of human geography, the norm against plural citizenship enforced community boundaries. As with territorial delimitation, under the old rule an individual was on one side of the line or the other; there was no straddling or overlap between communities. Territorial borders created spatial conjunctures—in the days before globalization, a border was consequential, in terms of social, cultural, and (of course) political development; a border even on a level field would amount to a barrier as important as a mountain. So, too, did the boundaries of citizenship. By minimizing overlap in state-based communities, the norm against dual nationality made those communities more distinct. That approach eliminated scalar [having a series of steps] possibilities, instead creating clear binary [based on two] arrangements which reinforced the sense of other in cross-community perceptions. A world in which the "us" and the "them" are rigidly separated is one in which both will loom larger. (Think sport teams and religions, and other institutions that demand exclusive loyalties.) In this respect, citizenship rules suppressing the incidence of dual nationality contributed to community identification. The rules were themselves consequential in a world that would otherwise lend itself to multiple, equivalent associations in the wake of immigration and lingering homeland ties.

Loyalty to One Nation May Become Uncommon

Acceptance of plural citizenship erodes this distinctiveness among national communities. As a matter of human geography, it becomes impossible to say where one community leaves off and another begins. A graphic representation of citizenship status would now be much more complex than a territorial map, characterized by overlapping spaces (especially tangled as triple nationality becomes more common) rather than separated ones. It is as if territory were to come under various joint regimes, in which more than one government exercised jurisdiction over the same piece of territory. (Indeed, insofar as territorial boundaries once represented, under the doctrine of sovereignty, zones of exclusive jurisdiction, those lines are also being blurred as various forms of trans- and supranational power emerge. Although our atlases may look basically the same, with the neat carving up of territory, the geographers of globalization are developing other maps to capture the new geography of power.) The arrangement is no longer binary; one can be both and many.

Plural citizenship may emerge a defining feature of a new era in which membership in states is demoted to the level of membership in other forms of association.

In short, plural citizenship saps national identity of its distinctiveness. If one can be American and also be Dominican or German or Filipino, it becomes more difficult to say what it means to be an American. That already presented enough of a challenge in the old world of singular nationality, but at least then it was more plausible to isolate the characteristics attaching to membership in the American polity to the exclusion of formal membership in other polities. What of assertions of a uniquely American creed when many citizens are not uniquely American? Plural citizenship emerges as another tool in the global infiltration of American ideals, in this case through the participation of American citizens as citizens in other political systems. But that infiltration undoes the identity as it loses differentiation. One can play on the old saying, "we have met the enemy and they is us," in unpacking the significance of plural citizenship. It is difficult to rally the "us" against a "them" when the two overlap. Attachment to state is no longer amenable [friendly] to loyalty tests. The need to choose between states no longer presents itself, as states themselves seem less competitive, not only for purposes of defense (a mostly obsolete function, at least against other states), but also for general community self-definition. The core is no longer distilled.

Again, this is offered as a matter of description, not lamentation. Nor, as with other citizenship practices that reflect a diminished national identity, is there anything really to be done about it. Into the next generation, as more children of mixed parentage and children of immigrants are able to sustain claims to alternate citizenship, plural citizenship may emerge a defining feature of a new era in which membership in states is demoted to the level of membership in other forms of association. As citizenship loses the sacral elements of exclusivity, it becomes just another form of belonging.

10

Dual Citizenship Does Not Mean Disloyalty

Paul Donnelly

Paul Donnelly is a writer and media consultant, with a 10-year record of promoting legal immigration, and is the organizer of the Web-based Immigration Reform Coalition.

Some Americans worry that dual citizenship creates divided loyalties. A U.S. citizen can have all sorts of loyalties and still remain true to his or her country, such as a spouse can remain faithful and yet love his or her mom and siblings. American identity is not based on ethnicity, language, culture, or economics, but on a civic faith—and if one possesses such a faith, why stop him or her from becoming an American citizen? In addition, there is the belief that all countries should recognize dual citizenship, because dual citizenship is only good if the rights and responsibilities of U.S. citizenship are extended with it. This goes with the idea that America is, as political commentator Ben Wattenberg put it, the "first universal nation," and that it is imperative that we continue to uphold this tradition.

A Mexican law that took effect in March [2000] allowing Mexican-Americans to claim "dual nationality" is an opportunity to ask profound questions about what it will mean to be an American citizen in the 21st century.

Mexico's motive is simple: There are millions of Mexican-Americans who are U.S. citizens, most of whom are middle

Peter Brimelow and Paul Donnelly, "Symposium," *Insight on the News*, vol. 16, July 3, 2000. Copyright © 2000 News World Communications, Inc. All rights reserved. Reproduced with permission of Insight.

class. The Mexican government would like these Americans to make investments in Mexico, create jobs and spend pesos. But Mexican governments long have shunned "foreign" involvement in their politics and economy.

So Mexico's new law allows those born in Mexico and naturalized in the United States to claim Mexican nationality but remain U.S. citizens. Like legal permanent residents of the United States (who are taxed on their worldwide income) they get economic rights and duties that only Mexicans have, but not political ones. They can vote for the mayor in Los Angeles but not in Juarez.

Dual Citizenship Does Not Threaten U.S. Citizenship

Some Americans worry about divided loyalties. But why should they? There is an almost feudal fear of modern freedom to travel and communicate—like the Afghani Islamic Taliban regime's death penalty for married women who talk to other men. It makes more sense to recognize that, just as a spouse can be faithful to his wife yet love his mom and sister (and even have female friends and coworkers), so too a U.S. citizen can have all sorts of loyalties—to America, Israel, the Baltimore Orioles, etc.

U.S. law and policy on dual citizenship is like the Mississippi River: powerful and muddy, but the direction is clear. It runs right down the heart of what it means to be an American. Unlike other countries, the United States was invented. When the Founders worked it out, there were no citizens anywhere on the planet; only subjects and sovereigns, rulers and ruled.

Core identity in most countries is founded on ethnicity, such as in Germany; or culture, as in France; or geography, as in Great Britain, historically an island possessed by the English, Welsh and Scots.

Our American identity, on the other hand, is not based on ethnicity, nor economics; not language or culture. America is based on a civic faith. Thomas Jefferson nailed the idea: "That all men are endowed by their Creator with certain unalienable rights and that to secure these rights, governments are instituted."

Dual citizenship hardly threatens U.S. citizenship. That is because, as [political commentator and writer] Ben Wattenberg put it, we are the "first universal nation." This partly explains why 65 million people from all over the world have come here. Complaints heard today about Mexican immigrants were heard in the 19th century about Germans, Irish and Italians. What worked then, works now: Americanization. They become us, and who we are expands to include them.

It makes more sense to recognize that, just as a spouse can be faithful to his wife yet love his mom and sister (and even have female friends and coworkers), so too a U.S. citizen can have all sorts of loyalties—to America, Israel, the Baltimore Orioles, etc.

The Bill of Rights exists within our borders, where our government keeps it secure. It does not dilute the universality of the American principles of freedom and self-government that other nations have followed our example. And it renews the sources of our liberties when immigrants come here to become Americans.

Unalienable Rights Reside in Individuals, Not the State

Dual citizenship is only possible when a U.S. citizen acquires another country's citizenship or when, as in the Mexican case, another nation's laws maintain a link with a person beyond their U.S. naturalization. Some object to that, citing the naturalization oath's phrase "I hereby renounce and abjure any and all foreign princes, potentates, states, or sovereignties." Those who swear the oath become U.S. citizens.

And yet, who cares what another country's laws say? That's not the mark of a confident nation. To understand American confidence over dual citizenship, consider when the federal government could take citizenship away: It cannot. We're a free country. Some of the Founders took the traditional European concept of the citizen as a subject—ergo, the state ruled. Jefferson took the opposite view—the individual is sovereign, not the state. The polity (all the citizens) make the state's decisions, but only to the point where unalienable rights reside in individuals: majority rule, minority rights.

Dual citizenship hardly threatens U.S. citizenship.

Look at the "Big Muddy": The world has at last adopted the American concept of citizenship, based on unalienable rights and individual sovereignty. They've followed our example of upholding individual liberties, and we should not subvert our tradition by attempting to punish those who choose dual citizenship.

Congress stirred the waters a bit by legislating "expatriating acts" by which a U.S. citizen lawfully abandons citizenship by actions such as voting in another country's elections serving in another country's armed forces or holding office in a foreign government. It is all to the good that these efforts to deny citizenship have been overturned by U.S. courts upholding the Constitution's founding promises.

The definitive statement was made in the *Afroyim vs. Rusk* decision in 1968. The State Department tried to enforce the statute that deemed voting in foreign elections was an expatriating act. The Supreme Court settled the matter: Congress has "no power" to deprive an American of his U.S. citizenship.

This was established by the case of the late Meir Kahane, founder of the Jewish Defense League in the United States and the Kach Party in Israel. Kach sent Kahane to the Knesset, Israel's parliament. The State Department informed him that serving in another nation's government would deprive him of his U.S. citizenship. Citing *Afroyim*, Kahane asserted that the State Department had no power to take his passport away. The court agreed. Kach's Israeli opponents outlawed those with dual citizenship from serving in the Knesset (Kahane voted in opposition). So to run for reelection, Kahane formally renounced his U.S. citizenship (he lost). When he re-entered the United States with his U.S. passport, the State Department again tried to take it away. The case went back to court, where the State Department lost again.

With some exasperation, the State Department pointed out that, after all, Kahane had renounced his citizenship. But Kahane's priceless response was, in effect: "Oh, I only did that because I had to, under Israeli law, to run for the Knesset. The U.S. government cannot deprive me of my U.S. citizenship— only I have that power and I do not choose to use it. I changed my mind." He won, and the State Department appealed. Kahane, however, was murdered while the appeal was pending and there the matter rests, as a matter of law. But as a matter of policy, some of us are waist-deep in the "Big Muddy."

Dual Citizenship Should Have Rights and Responsibilities of U.S. Citizenship

E Pluribus Unum [From Many, One] has a purpose. In 1999, Ghanian President Jerry Rawlings made a state visit to President [Bill] Clinton. At the press conference, a reporter asked: "I've heard that Ghana is offering some sort of dual citizenship to African-Americans. What's the reasoning behind it?" Rawlings replied: "You are our kith and kin." But the former dictator candidly stated the exclusive implications of citizenship: U.S citizenship "demand(s) loyalty to the American Constitution, and yet I cannot demand the same kind of loyalty to my country. But nonetheless, there's no reason why I will deny my fellow black African the right to enjoy the citizenship I enjoy as an African."

Clinton apparently thought Ghana's dual citizenship offer would be good for tourism, remarking that he thought it was "quite a clever idea." To his credit, Rawlings (who took power in a coup) then corrected Clinton about what being a Ghanaian means: Power. "[I]f you run afoul of the laws and regulations of my country, the—what do you call it?—the judiciary, the police and the laws of my country will take their cause without the American government attempting to intervene, to say, this is a citizen of my country." Inexcusably, Clinton agreed.

Consider the case of Harry Wu. A Chinese dissident, Wu spent years in the gulag [prison] and, upon becoming a U.S. citizen, returned to China to document atrocities such as organ farming. The Chinese arrested him, and the only reason he is still alive is that the U.S. government quietly told China: He's one of ours now. China does not recognize dual citizenship. Perhaps Ghana will persuade them to change.

Then there is Samuel Sheinbein. Showing no noticeable interest in being an Israeli before being accused of a particularly brutal murder in Montgomery County, Md., he then fled to Israel, which refused to extradite a dual U.S.-Israeli citizen. So Sheinbein was tried in Israel, convicted and received a lighter sentence than would have been likely in the community where the crime took place.

Surely, the president did not mean that crooks who claim dual citizenship with Ghana or any other country could simply switch passports, fly "home" and beat the rap. The Wu case shows that a U.S. passport remains a powerful shield, protecting the rights we founded our government to secure. Yet some governments, such as China's, hold that individuals are subjects still. What if, like Ghana, the Chinese authority that arrested Wu had "taken its course"?

So how about a simple principle: Dual citizenship is only good if the rights and responsibilities of U.S. citizenship are extended with it. If not, it's no good. Ghana is wrong: Citizenship isn't based on race. China is wrong: individual rights rule. Mexico is wrong: being Mexican (or Chinese or American or Ghanaian) isn't just about economic rights to invest, own and be taxed.

The Meaning of U.S. Citizenship

It may be argued that journalist Peter Brimelow, who was born in the United Kingdom, is living proof we need more civics in our naturalization test, since he managed to become a citizen without learning what it means to be an American. He's wrong to worry that immigrants who speak Spanish, or think fondly of the country they left behind, erode what makes us America. They renew it, instead.

The American model is the right one. That's why U.S. citizenship means so much, that so many will literally die for it. (Many with accents, and some with more than one passport.) We are always forming "the more perfect union." Let's keep it that way.

11

Dual-Language Programs Produce Bilingual Students

L. Lamor Williams

L. Lamor Williams is a reporter for Arkansas Online, a Web-based news outlet associated with the Arkansas Democrat-Gazette. *Previously Williams was a staff writer for the* Fort Worth Star-Telegram *in Fort Worth, Texas.*

Although they can be controversial, dual-language programs offer students an opportunity to become fluent in English without losing their native language skills; at the same time, these programs offer English speakers the chance to become fluent in another language—Spanish, for example—quickly. Although such programs require a huge commitment from students, parents, and teachers, the payoff can be even bigger when children become truly bilingual by fifth grade.

Mildred Vazquez's kindergartners know that a red tiger on the board means it's Spanish only, and a blue one means it's time to speak English.

"Escuchan!" Vazquez tells the students in the Academy at Carrie F. Thomas class. Listen!

This isn't English as a second language or a bilingual classroom. Some students speak English and some speak Spanish. But there is no translation. Students must figure out what Vazquez is saying based on her gestures and hints or get help from their classmates.

This "dual language" technique may seem harsh, but when applied correctly, educators say, it produces students who are bilingual by fifth grade and academically ahead of their peers.

Dual-language programs are gaining popularity in regions with high percentages of Hispanic students. In Tarrant County [Texas], five school districts—including Birdville, home of Carrie F. Thomas—have such programs.

The Arlington school district, where 16 percent of its 62,000 students are Hispanic in bilingual/ESL [English as a second language] classes, is looking at the program, said Gilda Evans, director of the district's bilingual/ESL department.

For years, educators have debated the merits of bilingual and English as a second language instruction versus total immersion.

The aim of these programs is to make non-English speakers fluent in English. But that approach can nearly eliminate a student's native language.

"In traditional bilingual or ESL classes, the primary language is squashed out," said Sabrina Lindsay, Carrie F. Thomas principal. "They may be able to speak it, but there's no literacy."

A dual-language classroom has English speakers and Spanish speakers. The curriculum is taught in both languages, and the goal is to produce bilingual students.

There are 231 registered dual-language programs in Texas, according to the Texas Two-Way/Dual Language Consortium, a group of educators that advocates for such programs.

David Silva, associate professor of linguistics at the University of Texas at Arlington, said the programs make Americans more competitive on the international stage and bring "us up to par with the rest of the world."

"In other parts of the world, it's a given that you speak at least two languages, if not three," Silva said.

In Vazquez's kindergarten class last year, Kevin Arce began the year speaking only Spanish. Jonathan Shier spoke only English.

Now first-graders, they recently returned to Vazquez's classroom to read in their second language to the new batch of kindergartners. Afterward, Vazquez quizzed her former students.

"Que es mama, Jonathan?" she said.

"Mom," he replied.

"Que es papa?"

"Daddy."

"Muy bien!" she said, giving him a high five.

There's no specific dual-language curriculum, so Vazquez must translate regular lesson plans for use in her classroom.

For dual language to be effective, Vazquez said, children must participate through fifth grade. They must also be kept together as a group. She requires each parent to sign a contract committing to the philosophy.

Lindsay said that as long as the parents remain in the district, their children will remain at Carrie F. Thomas at least through fifth grade.

Each student is tested before being admitted to the class and must demonstrate high proficiency in his or her native language.

"We build the foundation in their native language," Vazquez said. "In the second semester of first grade, we introduce them to reading and writing in the second language."

Of the six first-graders who qualified for gifted and talented classes at Carrie F. Thomas, five graduated from Vazquez's dual-language kindergarten class, Lindsay said.

"In some districts, only gifted students qualify for the dual-language programs because it requires extra training for the teachers and extra study time for the students so they can be on grade level or above in both languages," said Evans, who is researching the program for the Arlington school district.

The number of students enrolled in dual-language programs has doubled in the past decade. Statewide, 14.1 percent of 4.3 million students were enrolled in dual-language programs in 2003–04. That number was 7 percent of 3.6 million in the 1993–94 school year.

"Although it is a wonderful program design, it calls for more bilingual staff," Evans said.

Most area school districts are already on the prowl for bilingual teachers. In 2003, Arlington began offering $3,000 annual stipends to attract more bilingual teachers.

The bulk of Texas' dual-language programs are in regions with high percentages of Hispanic students, such as the Edinburg area of South Texas, which has 58 programs. The Houston area has 41, the El Paso region 35 and the San Antonio area 20.

More than 30 percent of the Fort Worth school district's 80,000 students are in bilingual classes—but they are focused on mastering English, not on preserving and expanding their knowledge of Spanish.

Fort Worth elementary schools have begun implementing a bilingual program in pre-kindergarten and kindergarten classes that uses a 50/50 concept in which half the instruction is given in English and half in Spanish, said Guadalupe Barreto, the district's elementary ESL coordinator.

Immersion programs are typically a last resort for districts, usually because parents have refused bilingual or ESL services. Such programs place Spanish-speaking students in English-speaking classes, and the children must sink or swim.

ESL teachers rely heavily on pictures and nonverbal communication techniques to teach students from various linguistic backgrounds simultaneously.

"In this part of the world, there are Hispanic students and Vietnamese students, for example, who don't speak their native languages even though their parents and grandparents might," Silva said. "There is a fair amount of stigma and pressure for them to speak English."

Lindsay said her school's demographics began changing about two years ago to include more Hispanic students. Today, the school is about 22 percent Hispanic.

Lindsay said initially she wanted to find the best way to educate her Spanish-speaking youngsters.

In May 2004, Lindsay and other school district officials visited Mesita Elementary School in El Paso to observe the dual-language concept.

"I was just blown away," Lindsay said. "The kids were actually bilingual, and it was apparent in everything they were doing. I immediately said we have to have it on this campus."

Birdville administrators helped her put together a plan, and the program began last fall.

Now the waiting list for the program at Carrie F. Thomas has a dozen names. Two dual-language kindergarten classes are planned for next year, Lindsay said.

Vazquez will teach the Spanish portion of the class and a second teacher will teach the English portion, Lindsay said.

Vazquez's current students are learning numbers, the alphabet and the days of the week through songs in English and Spanish.

To learn the months, they sing and dance, Enero, Febrero, Marzo, Abril . . . to the 1990s dance tune "Macarena."

"Otra!" Vazquez says.

"Si!" the children reply, launching into the song.

"Escuchan!" Vazquez says. And the wiggling begins again.

12

Bilingual Societies Remain Tense and Divided

Richard D. Lamm

A politician and lawyer, Richard D. Lamm is the former governor of Colorado. He wrote the book, Immigration Time Bomb: The Fragmenting of America. *He also is chairman of the advisory board of the Federation for American Immigration Reform (FAIR), an anti-illegal immigration group.*

A country that emphasizes its bilingual/bicultural aspects will ultimately fragment. Having no common language, purpose, or ideals breeds balkanization, or the violent isolation and segmentation experienced in multiethnic regions such as the former Soviet Union. All citizens of the United States must share a sense of common destiny and fate with one another regardless of their ethnicity. Speaking a common language and espousing common ideas is the way past immigrants assimilated and achieved this sense of unity with other Americans, and its the way the rising numbers of immigrants must do so today.

Americans have an almost blind faith in the melting pot. Not without reason. Our greatest national achievement is fashioning a common identity out of a wide variety of races, nationalities and ethnic groups.

The melting pot melted and we became (with a few lumps) one nation and one people. We did not create a perfect world, but we became a unified nation with a common identity, common language and common allegiances. *E Pluribus Unum* (From Many, One) is both a promise and a challenge.

Today, that unity is at risk. Immigrants make up more than 10 percent of our population, which has only happened once before in our history, and they are disproportionately Spanish-speakers who can (and do) maintain contact with the old country. We have never taken so disproportionate an amount of immigrants from one linguistic group.

America Must Insist on Allegiance

Meanwhile, our own assimilative demands have also been dramatically reduced. Arthur M. Schlesinger Jr., [American historian and] one of the great liberals of my lifetime, warned: "Ethnic ideologies have set themselves against the old American ideal of assimilation. They call on this republic to think in terms not of individual but group identity and to move the policy from individual to group rights. They have made a certain progress in transforming the United States into a more segregated society. They have filled the air with recrimination and rancor and have remarkably advanced the fragmentation of America."

So the numbers, the proximity, the incessant flow of Spanish-speaking immigrants, year after year, are building up a bilingual, bicultural society within our society. The tradition that people would drop old loyalties and join us in our polity [political organization] is disappearing under these pressures. Now some immigrants can vote for both president of Mexico and president of the United States (the latter in either English or Spanish), and we have abandoned the idea that we "foreswear all other allegiances."

We are backing into becoming a bilingual, bicultural society despite the fact that there are no happy models out there. Belgium is talking about splitting its 1,000-year-old country because of the tension produced by its bilingual/bicultural society. Quebec talks about independence from Canada. In Spain, different language groups set off deadly bombs to force more autonomy. India, Sri Lanka, Malaysia, Madagascar and numerous other countries are suppressing rebellion by minority cultural groups. Bilingual/bicultural nations seem to be inherently unstable. Switzerland has a distinct and separate French, German and Roma speaking sections, which is hardly an encouraging example.

Citizens Share the Fate of Their Neighbors

I would suggest that our Founders got it right and we abandon our assimilative model of nation-building at our great risk. We have to start to give serious consideration to what policies allow us to form community, live at peace with our neighbors and avoid fragmentation and balkanization [the process of a region breaking into small, often hostile units].

We do not bond automatically to our neighbors. In many parts of the world, neighbors are viewed as strangers and competitors. A cohesive nation needs a shared stake in the future. It needs a shared language, shared culture, shared norms and values. It needs common goals and common dreams. Nations are forged by commitment, dedication, hard work, tolerance, love and a search for commonalties.

We are backing into becoming a bilingual, bicultural society despite the fact that there are no happy models out there.

It must understand that all members to a certain degree have a shared fate. To say my fate is not tied to your fate is like saying, "Your end of the boat is sinking." A peaceful nation needs, in short, a unifying social glue, including (but not limited to) a common language.

America's first Puerto Rican-born congressman, Herman Badillo, was the chief sponsor of the Federal Bilingual Education legislation. He now repents his sponsorship because it is balkanizing and "hurts students more than it helps." He warns against a bilingual/bicultural society and demands that Hispanics learn English and "be held to the same high standards as all other Americans."

We can be multi-ethnic but we must have a common language and common culture. We must stay "one nation indivisible."

A sign in a New York classroom late last century warned "Learn English. Be American. Otherwise America will become like the old country."

We are in the process of ignoring that wise advice. What could be the next generation of immigrant success stories is instead bringing a whole second language group to the United States, with its own separate mores, values and culture. We risk instead of having new Americans, having instead "Mexicans living in America" and all history shows that is a prescription for "turmoil, tension and tragedy."

13

The English Language Is Not Endangered

Leonard Pitts Jr.

Leonard Pitts is a nationally syndicated columnist for the Miami Herald, *and he won the Pulitzer Prize for Commentary in 2004. He primarily writes about race, politics, and culture in America.*

Advertising in Spanish does not endanger the supremacy of English and does not discourage immigrants from learning it. In fact, English is unlikely ever to lose its position as the primary language of the United States. Fears of English being usurped by Spanish reveal an inflexibility and basic unwillingness to admit that the ethnic makeup of the American population is in flux. In fact, it always has been.

La gente dice que Earl Stewart lo hizo solo por el poderoso dolar.

(People say Earl Stewart did it only for the almighty dollar.)

El dice que tienen razon.

(He says they're right.)

What's that? The subtitles are distracting? Fine, I'll stop.

But the point here is, all Stewart wanted to do was sell Toyotas. It's something he's been doing for 33 years as the proprietor of Earl Stewart Toyota in Palm Beach County [Florida]. Then he hit upon an idea he thought might expand his market: Spanish-language commercials with English subtitles. The spots run on English-language television and, though he speaks no Spanish, Stewart stars in them himself.

The subtitles, he says, were an afterthought. "I said, 'You know, I'm going to be talking to a lot of people that don't speak Spanish so, as a courtesy or to explain what I'm doing, maybe I should use English subtitles.' It was really an effort on my part, albeit a failure, to be nice to the monolingual folks."

The "monolingual folks" were not feeling the love—putting it mildly. Stewart says the commercial brought him a "flood" of angry, often profane e-mails and phone calls, nine out of every 10 sharply critical of his commercial. As described by Stewart, the complaints tended to be longer on emotion than on logic.

The Monoliguists' Fear Is Ungrounded

For instance, they said that by advertising in Spanish, he encouraged Spanish-speakers to avoid learning English. But he was advertising on English stations, so anyone watching presumably already spoke the language.

And people kept referencing Mexico, usually in sentences that began with, "Why don't you go back to . . ." But anybody who knows South Florida knows that, while it is home to many Spanish speakers, the bulk of them are not Mexican.

"I think there's a lot of fear out there," says Stewart. "All of the (2008 presidential) candidates to some extent are using the immigration thing as a lever to get elected. They're appealing to the fear Americans have, some of this 9/11 stuff. And the rhetoric has a lot of the people who are not as informed or maybe don't listen carefully, convinced that most of the Spanish people in this country are illegal immigrants or they're terrorists."

It's a cogent [intellectually compelling] analysis, but I think there's more going on here. One suspects that at bottom what set Stewart's critics off is a fear so visceral they might not even have words to express it. Put simply: Since when do we need subtitles in our own country?

To which the best answer is probably another question. Who is "we"? What is "our"?

It's exceedingly unlikely that English is in danger of losing its position of primacy [in the United States].

The fact is that "we" is not what it used to be, and "our" reflects a nation more diverse than ever before. The Census Bureau says the Hispanic population of Palm Beach County stands at 16.7 percent, nearly two percentage points higher than the national figure. Isn't it smart business to reach out to them? Why begrudge Stewart's efforts to do so?

Change Can Be Scary But It Is Inevitable

Granted, it's not hard to empathize with the sense of dislocation some people feel as they watch the nation changing around them. But to understand what they feel is not necessarily to share it.

In the first place, hysterical predictions to the contrary notwithstanding, it's exceedingly unlikely that English is in danger of losing its position of primacy. In the second place, people will sooner or later have to understand that while change is frightening, change is also life, especially in a nation as susceptible as this one to the forces of the free market. Which is, for my money, the moral of Stewart's story.

He says that as that story has become better known, the public response has done a 180-degree turnabout. The commercial—and the notoriety—have brought customers from as far away as Miami. And he's just had his best September, ever. All of which leaves Stewart with mixed emotions. He's disappointed in many of his fellow Americans.

On the other hand, business is good.

14

A Diverse America Can Be United

Stewart David Ikeda

Novelist and non-fiction writer Stewart David Ikeda is editor-in-chief of IMDiversity.com, a Web site advocating multiculturalism.

Barack Obama is more than black, and, as President of the United States, he represents more than only black citizens. In fact, as a product of several ethnic backgrounds, President Obama reflects the true diversity of America. He is a living, breathing example of America's success at assimilation. But not everyone sees his election in such a positive light. Many whites fear that in the interest of diversity, Mr. Obama will exclude them. They see diversity as code for opposition to whites rather than as advocacy for all races and ethnicities. If they understand that opposition to mean, however, that whites will no longer have ultimate authority by virtue of the color of their skin, their fears are grounded. Until all people view each other as equals amid difference, our unity as a nation will remain an illusion.

On this day after an election [November 5, 2008] that has seen every form of description—"historic", "epic", "unprecedented", "seachange", etc.—punditry and surveys and Twitters and number-crunching will abound. Analyses will be piled atop analyses for days, weeks, or months to come—maybe longer.

And this prolonged social moment we've been through *is* all those things—unprecedented, historic, and indubitably [undoubtedly] worthy of very careful counting, parsing [carefully examining], and reflection upon what we've just seen.

That said, one immediate implication of this election's final days and result goes to the very heart of this publication's meaning and mission—the recognition and championing of diversity as the strength of America.

Obama's victory is a clear vindication of the argument for diversity, and not only in the relatively limited sense of representational politics. Yes, that he "happens to be" Black, or half-Black, and as such fulfills the once-unimaginable aspirations of a country haunted by a racist past, *is* momentous. However, it is probably of more psychological importance to *us*—to the electorate—than it will be for Obama in leading us.

Obama Is More Than Black

To call Obama the first Black president is something of a misnomer, and it is tokenizing [making symbolic efforts rather than real efforts]. It would be tokenizing to assume that he will, by himself, "part the seas" and correct all the uglier aspects of race relations in America. The hopes and expectations Obama's supporters have laid on him are hefty. And while his accomplishment is inspiring, he will have weightier items on his agenda on Day One than to sit basking in the fact of being the first half-Black president. On the other side, already, anti-Affirmative Action pundits have also been tokenizing Obama, using his ascent to deny racial disparities and inequities throughout American society, from schools to healthcare coverage to the work place.

As [African American minister and politician] Al Sharpton recently observed on CNN's D.L. Hughley show, the particular alchemy of Obama's *mixed* background is what makes him a well-suited figurehead for our times and our diverse country. He will be the White President and the Black president and the Brown president, Sharpton said, and he will have to *per-*

form to lead us out of the crises, domestic and foreign, our still largely divided nation faces.

But the importance of Obama's background and feat is more symbolic, subtle and complex than it is literal. It's in how he won and in the movement he inspired. First, he ran a campaign that attempted to sidestep, and to "transcend" race, and that succeeded insofar as he did not "play the race card," even when the opposition attempted to wield voters' race fear against them—a tactic that thankfully failed, for once and at last, to win the day. Second, he never allowed himself to be "the Black candidate"—initially to the dismay of some Black voters and commentators. He always presented himself as multiracial, product of a multicultural family, a global-era family, raised as a *"hapa"* [a Hawaiian of mixed race] in the most multicultural of states, and routinely pictured against the backdrop of his white mother and grandparents, his Asian siblings, with his Midwestern constituents. Third, his election was possible only through creation of an effective multicultural, multiracial coalition of supporters that reflected the emergent "New America Majority" predicted since the 2000 Census, but slow to represent itself at the ballot box.

[Barack Obama] will be the White President and the Black president and the Brown president.

He built a campaign that was as diverse as this country, and where everyone could "claim" a piece of the candidate and the future. He led a largely transformed Democratic Party, marked and revitalized by unprecedented diversity. This was evidenced in its 50-state strategy, its slate of presidential and state candidates this year, its investment in minority outreach, and even more obviously at the convention. In Denver this year [at the 2008 Democratic National Convention], and on the campaign trail with Obama, we saw a picture of us as we are—the *real* America, which was very different from the one that the likes of defeated Virginia senator George Allen, and [2008 Republican vice-presidential candidate] Sarah Palin, tried to sell us.

Many Fear Obama's Success

Not everyone liked what they saw, and this election showed us that with great change comes great *anxiety*. The uglier threads in this campaign season—from the primaries right up to the booing at John McCain's concession speech—showed that race, gender, religious and class tensions among us are real and palpable, even as they are becoming more difficult to discuss explicitly. For many Americans, Obama's victory symbolizes that we are living in a "new" country whose rules may not be familiar. Some opponents have worried aloud about political suppression, a concern over being able to criticize Obama for fear of "political correctness" or being branded "racist".

This day after the history-making election of Barack Obama as our first not-wholly-white president leaves us to face an overwhelming question: *Now what?*

Some Americans accustomed to—and expecting to—always and only seeing themselves at the head of the table may find it difficult for a while coming back into the room and figuring out where to sit. But what sober Obama's acceptance speech underscored last night is that at his table, everyone will be welcome—and needed. And it is up to those hesitant Americans to find the resolve and purpose to overcome their natural apprehension and take a seat.

"Diversity" is not code for "non-whites-only"; "diversity" means "diversity."

This is a similar phenomenon to one that we've observed over the years of publishing this site [IMDiversity.com], where occasionally—not often, but a few times a year, perhaps—the editors will receive a flame message raging against the audience structure of this site network, condemning us for "excluding whites," charging a "reverse-racism," demanding "where's the *White* Village"? This is a false position that sees "diversity" as oppositional to "whiteness"; it sees work opportunity as a zero-sum game, and *equal* opportunity as oppositional to white-opportunity. Because it does not adhere to the old rules, positioning whiteness as the default center of the experience, it is presumed to be exclusive. It too seems to say, *If I can't be at the head of the table, I'm not sitting.*

Diversity Means Everyone

The editors take these concerns seriously, and for many years attempted to address them both through our content and direct correspondence when possible (they are almost always anonymous). We try to explain that the founding purpose of this site was to represent the concerns and interests of underrepresented minorities in the U.S. workforce, including women, those who faced specific discriminations and protections. We also seek to help employers interested in providing equal opportunity and building a diverse workforce to present open opportunities to these groups. We stress that the opportunities presented here are not jobs set aside for or open exclusively to these groups, and that we encourage any qualified candidate to apply to the jobs. We also point out that whites are well-represented in our staff, leadership teams, prominent contributors and business partners, article subjects and readers. We observe that among those who do make use of our free, open job seeker tools and apply for jobs are users of all backgrounds, regions and abilities, including high numbers of users who choose to self-identify (ethnic self-identification is encouraged but strictly optional on our site) as "Caucasian/white". We argue that "diversity" is not code for "non-whites-only"; "diversity" means "diversity." Those who have ears to hear sometimes engage with us appreciatively, write us back and participate as users in the site, but it's not satisfactory for everyone. Some must come around to it on their own.

Barack Obama's huge victory illustrates what the most progressive employers and users of this site have known for some time, but writ large: that investing in diversity is not a matter of parsing, tokenizing and dividing for any "politically correct" purpose, but a competitive imperative in the "new America" and the shrinking global village. It makes sense and it works.

It is to the credit of both presidential candidates that on election eve, they attempted to deliver a message of concilia-tion, unity and seriousness of purpose in moving forward to tackle the country's problems. But unlike the past eight years, in which "unity" served as code for homogeneity and towing a party line, in the Obama era, unity will be achieved through our variety and the strength of our differences. Out of many, one. *e Pluribus Unum.*

That is diversity.

15

Businesses Must Market to a Diverse Society

Esther Novak

Peruvian-born Esther Novak is a member of New Jersey Governor Jon Corzine's Council for Economic Growth. In 2006, she was named the Professional Services Business Person of the Year by the Statewide Hispanic Chamber of Commerce of New Jersey. She is on the board of directors of the Association of Hispanic Advertising Agencies.

Corporate leaders would do well to learn a crucial lesson from President Barack Obama. To appeal to the entire country, you must appeal to the diverse mix of people who now call themselves American. Also, you must speak to each group in the unique way they prefer. The days when marketers could offer slight nods to "ethnic diversity" are gone. Savvy companies will identify each group's unique desires and needs and directly address them. Those who refuse to do so risk losing money from the ever-increasing, non-white segments of American society.

The recent election has probably settled one long-standing debate: It's worth investing in multicultural markets, whether to win a political campaign or business revenue.

In fact, the success of President-elect Barack Obama's campaign provides a case study for building a brand with appeal to nearly every demographic segment of American society. Two pieces of data that clearly informed Obama and his advisers as they plotted their campaign strategy are noteworthy of note for all C-suite residents, because they tackled them flawlessly.

First, as the U.S. Census has been showing for some time, we are an incredibly diverse nation—the ultimate "stew" of ingredients from every nationality, race, and creed. Second, the various segments of our population don't respond to a one-size-fits-all approach, whether it's getting out the vote or selling diapers. People respond to appreciation for their individuality, and when reached through their preferred channels.

Learning From Marketing 101

You might think this is first-year theory for any business-school student. And you might think your business is already addressing these needs within the multicultural market segments within your corporate "diversity" program.

Yes, a number of companies claim to address "special interest" communities—African, Asian, and Hispanic Americans; gay, lesbian, bisexual, and transgender individuals; Native Americans; disabled citizens; senior citizens; women. Some add other groups to this list, such as Arab Americans, veterans, etc.

However, for many companies, their approaches to these markets mainly arose from legal requirements such as Affirmative Action and Equal Employment Opportunity. While such measures drove a measure of progress toward inclusion, four decades later, sophisticated understanding of these markets and their consumers' behavior seems to have flown past the world view of many marketing departments.

Cultivating Cultural Savvy

To put it simply, merely including images of diverse peoples or translating some marketing materials into another language does not constitute an effective approach to potential customers of diverse cultures. Instead, savvy business leaders can help their teams understand that the market is more varied and nuanced—a richer version of America the Beautiful—than at first glance.

So, what insights should we bear in mind when considering multicultural markets? Start with these facts:

- About one in three U.S. residents is a minority. In fact, the minority population in the U.S. is larger than the total population of all but 11 countries.

- Minorities don't just live in urban areas. Nearly one in 10 U.S. counties is "majority-minority," having more than 50% minority residents, according to data released by the Census Bureau last August. As of July 2007, 302 of the nation's 3,141 counties had more people identifying themselves as non-white than those that labeled themselves white.

- Minority populations have more buying power and a bigger middle-class and affluent sector than you may realize. The University of Georgia's Selig Center for Economic Growth reports that the buying power of Hispanics exceeded $860 billion in 2007 and will grow to more than $1.2 trillion five years from now. For the same period, African-Americans spent $845 billion with growth, to $1.1 trillion in five years, and Asian-Americans $459 billion, with growth projected to rise to $670 billion.

- Core values and behavior are even more important than language when it comes to marketing to multicultural America. These include the role of family, connection to home country, respect for the elderly, the influence of community leaders, and the roles of faith, tradition, and cultural icons.

Additionally, for many first- and second-generation immigrants, acculturation has taken precedence over assimilation.

The ability to retain core values while living in a dominant culture has trumped the old model of shedding native language and customs. "Commonalities" such as preference for emotional connection, grassroots, or digital communication, can be leveraged across multicultural segments for marketing efficiency and effectiveness.

Multicultural Stimulus

I'm not an economist, but I can guarantee you that when it comes time to "sell" a stimulus plan to the American public, the Obama administration will use the same kind of approach to America's diverse audiences it did in the campaign. Residents of Portuguese background in Newark's Ironbound district will hear about its benefits in their local papers and ward leaders; Vietnamese-Americans in Houston will likely receive face-to-face briefings in community center meetings; African-Americans in Los Angeles may hear talk of the plan from the pulpits of their churches.

Additionally, the 10 million people with e-mail addresses in the Obama campaign database will be segmented, with messaging tailored to each cultural, ethnic and demographic group. Every venue, channel, social media platform, and messenger will be tapped to bolster the plan, whether it's the press, the Web, advertising, rallies, events, you name it, all filtering up toward local, county, state, and federal policymakers.

But it won't just be about delivering a message to targeted groups. The incoming Administration is sure to have "eyes and ears" responsible for identifying and assessing each group's needs, wants, and priorities—and striving, as much as possible, to find ways of showing how the stimulus package will address them. It will be a complex, often nonlinear process, and probably a good test of the President-elect and his team's discipline. In the end, however, the Administration will need to connect emotionally with diverse America, linking their values and dreams with policy and legislation that brings them out of the economic crisis.

Such a process is worth thinking about the next time you—whether a CEO, an entrepreneur, a manager, or the next U.S. President—deliver a speech, introduce a new product or idea, or appeal to your customers, investors, employees, or target audience.

Understanding the nuances of this great nation's many cultures, and adopting strategies to address them on their terms, can help open or advance a company's fortunes, and perhaps even give it a first-mover advantage with these brand-loyal markets—just as a certain savvy candidate did on Nov. 4.

Organizations to Contact

The editors have compiled the following list of organizations concerned with the issues debated in this book. The descriptions are derived from materials provided by the organizations. All have publications or information available for interested readers. The list was compiled on the date of publication of the present volume; the information provided here may change. Be aware that many organizations take several weeks or longer to respond to inquiries, so allow as much time as possible.

American Civil Liberties Union (ACLU)
125 Broad St., 18th Fl., New York, NY   10004
Web site: www.aclu.org

Founded in 1920, the ACLU works in courts, legislatures and communities to defend and preserve individual rights and liberties guaranteed by the Constitution and laws of the United States. The ACLU has been one of the nation's leading advocates for the rights of immigrants, refugees, and non-citizens, challenging unconstitutional laws and practices and countering what it sees as the myths upon which many of these laws are based. The ACLU believes that when the government denies rights to immigrants in this country, it denies rights to all. The ACLU's Web site provides a news feed of relevant immigration stories, and it covers immigrant-related issues on its Blog of Rights. Recent publications include *Immigration Myths and Facts* and *Conditions of Confinement in Immigrant Detention Facilities.*

American Immigration Control Foundation
PO Box 525, Monterey, VA   24465
(540) 468-2022
Web site: www.aicfoundation.com

Founded in 1983, the American Immigration Control Foundation is a nonprofit research and educational organization that aims to inform Americans of the need for a reasonable immigration policy based on the nation's interests and capacity to assimilate newcomers. Its Web site includes books, booklets, pamphlets, and videos for purchase. Recent publications include *Erasing America—The Politics of the Borderless Nation* and *Immigration and the Public Health Crisis.*

National Association for Bilingual Education (NABE)
1313 L St. NW, Ste. 210, Washington, DC   20005
(202) 898-1829
Web site: www.nabe.org

The National Association for Bilingual Education is a professional organization devoted to representing both English-language learners and bilingual education professionals. The organization is made up of more than 20,000 bilingual and English-as-a-second-language teachers, administrators, paraprofessionals, university professors and students, researchers, advocates, policy makers, and parents. Back issues of NABE publications, including its *Bilingual Research Journal* and *NABE News* magazine, are available on the Web site.

National Immigration Forum
50 F St. NW, Ste. 300, Washington, DC   20001
(202) 347-0040
Web site: www.immigrationforum.org

The National Immigration Forum is an organization dedicated to embracing and upholding America's tradition as a nation of immigrants. Founded in 1982, it is the leading immigrant advocacy group in the United States. Its Web site provides various fact sheets, backgrounders, legislative analysis briefs, issue papers, and other documents related to immigration. Recent publications include *Assets or Enemies: Securing our Nation by Enforcing Immigration Laws* and *Summaries of Recent Reports on Immigration Detention, 2007–2009.*

U.S. Department of Homeland Security

U.S. Department of Homeland Security
Washington, DC   20528
(202) 282-8000
Web site: www.dhs.gov

The Department of Homeland Security is responsible for providing immigration-related services and benefits such as naturalization and work authorization as well as investigative and enforcement responsibilities for enforcement of federal immigration laws, customs laws, and air security laws. The Web site provides press releases as well as statistics and other information related to immigration.

U.S. ENGLISH, Inc.

1747 Pennsylvania Ave. NW, Ste. 1050
Washington, DC   20006
(202) 833-0100
Web site: www.us-english.org

U.S. ENGLISH, Inc. is dedicated to preserving the unifying role of the English language in the United States. It was founded in 1983 by the late Senator and immigrant, S.I. Hayakawa, and has 1.8 million members. Links to relevant pending immigration legislation may be accessed through the organization's Web site. The Web site also offers e-alerts featuring updates on official English legislation in Congress and in individual states as well as links to the organization's quarterly newsletter, *U.S. ENGLISH Report.*

Workplace Fairness

2031 Florida Ave. NW, Ste. 500, Washington, DC   20009
(202) 243-7660
Web site: www.workplacefairness.org

Workplace Fairness is a nonprofit organization that provides information, education, and assistance to individual workers and their advocates nationwide, and it also promotes public policies that advance employee rights, including those of immigrants. Founded in 1994, the organization was originally called the National Employee Rights Institute (NERI). The organization's Web site offers a wide variety of resources, including a section highlighting relevant workplace facts and statistics as well as books, reports, and articles. The Workplace Fairness free e-newsletter contains a week's worth of news stories and court cases affecting employees and their advocates, plus a link to the organization's award-winning blog, *Today's Workplace.*

Bibliography

Books

Christa Davis
Acampora and
Angela L. Cotton,
ed.
Unmaking Race, Remaking Soul: Transformative Aesthetics and the Practice of Freedom. Albany, NY: State University of New York Press, 2007.

Michael Barone
New Americans: How the Melting Pot Can Work Again. Washington, DC: Regnery Publishers, 2001.

Elzbieta M.
Gozdziak and
Susan F. Martin,
ed.
Beyond the Gateway: Immigrants in a Changing America. Lanham, MD: Lexington Books, 2005.

Samuel P.
Huntington
Who Are We? The Challenges to America's National Identity. New York: Simon & Schuster, 2004.

Young Yun Kim
Becoming Intercultural: An Integrative Theory of Communication and Cross-Cultural Adaptation. Thousand Oaks, CA: Sage Publications, 2001.

Desmond King
The Liberty of Strangers: Making the American Nation. New York: Oxford University Press, 2005.

Robert A. Levine
Assimilating Immigrants: Why America and France Cannot. Santa Monica, CA: RAND, 2004.

Gregory Rodriguez — *Mongrels, Bastards, Orphans and Vagabonds: Mexican Immigration and the Future of Race in America.* New York: Random House, 2007.

Anne Tyler — *Digging to America.* New York: Alfred A. Knopf, 2006.

Cornel West — *Race Matters.* Boston: Beacon Press, 2001.

Teresa Williams-León and Cynthia L. Nakashima — *Sum of Our Parts: Mixed-Heritage Asian Americans.* Philadelphia: Temple University Press, 2001.

Periodicals

Elizabeth Aguilera — "The Latino Landscape: Assimilation, Separation," *Denver Post,* July 20, 2004.

Danielle Dimartino — "One on One: Getting Up Close on Immigration," *Dallas Morning News,* August 2, 2006.

Peter Duignan — "Bilingual Education: A Critique," *Hoover Institution,* September 25, 1998. www.hooverinstitution.org.

Nick Gillespie — "The Decline of the English Speaking Peoples: America's National Language Is Under Seige," *Reason,* July 2006.

Thomas Hill — "Bush Opposes Latino Integration," *The America's Intelligence Wire,* May 2, 2006.

S.A. Miller and Jon Ward — "Emphasis on English: Assimiliation Seen as Vital for Immigrants' Success," *The Washington Times*, March 13, 2005.

Nashville City Paper — "Opposition to English Only Needs to Be Heard," October 20, 2008.

Ruben Navarrette, Jr. — "The Great Language Debate," *San Diego Union Tribune*, December 5, 2007.

Filimon Peonidis — "Four Questions to Will Kymlicka: Multiculturalism and Liberal Democracy," *Eurozine*, July 25, 2008. www.eurozine.com.

Leonard Pitts — "No Matter How You Say It, English-only Idea's Silly," *The Houston Chronicle*, May 22, 2006.

Robert Samuelson — "The Hard Truth of Immigration," *Newsweek*, June 13, 2005.

San Diego Union-Tribune — "Evidence Growing: Studies Show Immigrants Are Assimilating," May 14, 2008.

William Underhill — "The Melting of the Melting Pot," *Newsweek International*, January 5, 2009.

Shankar Vedantam — "Why the Ideological Melting Pot Is Getting So Lumpy," *Washington Post*, January 19, 2009.

Washington Times — "Keep Dreaming," October 26, 2007.

Rebecca Weber   "English-Only Laws Are Restricting
More than Just What's Being Said,"
National Education Association,
November 1, 2006. www.nea.org.

Index

DATE DUE

MAR 07 2012			

DEMCO 38-296